The Homework Series

Mathematics A7

Published by Solomon Press
PO Box 3867
BATH BA1 7TY

Tel: 01225 852238

E-mail: info@solomon-press.com
Website: www.solomon-press.com

The Homework Series is a trade mark of Solomon Press

© J Dawe E Garrett E Morgan 1997
First published 1997
Ninth reprint 2007
Second edition 2000 (Revised for *Framework for teaching mathematics: Year 7*)

ISBN 1 901724 00 X
ISBN 978-1-901724-004

All rights reserved
No part of this publication may be reproduced,
stored in a retrieval system, or transmitted in
any form or by any means without the prior
written permission of Solomon Press

Design and typesetting by Pedeke Ltd, Bridgwater, Somerset
Printed in Great Britain by Sprint Print, Exeter, Devon

Contents

Calculation & the Number System

N1	Whole number calculations	....	4
N2	Whole number word problems	....	4
N3	Factors, multiples and primes	....	4
N4	Rounding whole numbers	....	5
N5	Approximating answers	....	5
N6	BODMAS	....	6
N7	Place value in decimals	....	6
N8	Calculating with decimals A	....	7
N9	Calculating with decimals B	....	8
N10	Decimals - including rounding	....	8
N11	Money calculations	....	8
N12	Negative numbers	....	9
N13	Fractional parts	....	10
N14	Calculating with fractions	....	11
N15	Equivalent fractions, lowest terms	....	11
N16	Ratio and proportion	....	12
N17	Fractions, percentages, decimals	....	12
N18	Using percentages	....	13

Algebra

A1	Sequences	....	14
A2	Number machines	....	14
A3	Writing formulas	....	16
A4	Using formulas	....	16
A5	Collecting like terms	....	17
A6	Substituting in expressions	....	18
A7	Co-ordinates and graphs	....	18
A8	Solving equations	....	19
A9	Equations, trial and improvement	....	20
A10	Solving equations using inverses	....	20

Shape, Space and Measures

S1	Co-ordinates in the first quadrant	....	21
S2	Co-ordinates in all four quadrants	....	21
S3	Polygons and congruent shapes	....	22
S4	Reflection	....	22
S5	Line symmetry	....	23
S6	Rotational symmetry	....	23
S7	Angles - measuring and naming	....	24
S8	Angles and lines	....	25
S9	Angle sum of triangles	....	25
S10	Constructing triangles	....	26
S11	Rectangles - areas and perimeters	....	27
S12	Areas of triangles	....	27
S13	Areas of compound shapes	....	28
S14	Naming solids	....	29
S15	Nets of solids	....	30
S16	Surface area of cuboids	....	30
S17	2D – 3D visualisation	....	31
S18	Conversions between units	....	31
S19	Units of measurement	....	32
S20	Rotation	....	32
S21	Scales and dials	....	33
S22	Time	....	34
S23	Time and timetables	....	35
S24	Translations	....	35

Handling Data

D1	Surveys and tallying	....	36
D2	Grouped data	....	37
D3	Bar charts and bar-line graphs	....	38
D4	Bar charts and line graphs	....	38
D5	Pictograms	....	39
D6	Interpreting pie charts	....	40
D7	Misleading diagrams	....	41
D8	Mean and mode	....	42
D9	Median and range	....	43
D10	Simple scatter diagrams	....	44
D11	Likelihood and chance	....	44
D12	Chance and probability	....	45

Revision & Solving Problems

R1	Number	....	46
R2	Number	....	46
R3	Number	....	47
R4	Algebra	....	47
R5	Algebra	....	48
R6	Algebra	....	48
R7	Shape, space and measures	....	48
R8	Shape, space and measures	....	49
R9	Shape, space and measures	....	50
R10	Handling data	....	51
R11	Handling data	....	52
R12	Handling data	....	53
R13	Mixed problems	....	54
R14	Mixed problems	....	54
R15	Mixed problems	....	55
R16	Mixed problems	....	56
R17	Mixed problems	....	56

Calculations and the Number System

Homework N1

Do not use a calculator for this homework

1. **a** 357 + 1088 **b** 126 + 34 + 1903
   c 19 588 + 766 **d** 1098 + 375 + 6 + 48
   e 58 + 1807 + 359 + 12 + 23 040 + 7

2. **a** 128 − 75 **b** 1022 − 574
   c 2505 − 766 **d** 10 101 − 3284
   e 3 002 021 − 764 538

3. **a** 27 × 18 **b** 58 × 43
   c 1898 × 6 **d** 165 × 14
   e 185 × 283 **f** 1054 × 162

4. **a** 188 ÷ 4 **b** 296 ÷ 8
   c 29 645 ÷ 7 **d** 10 026 ÷ 6
   e 5556 ÷ 12

5. **a** 257 + 554 − 687 **b** 8506 + 18 − 767
   c 1009 − 779 + 182 **d** 100 000 − 16 + 31
   e 2575 + 30 892 − 16 701 − 8306 − 12

Homework N2

1. What number is 67 less than two million?

2. What is one hundred and fifty thousand more than three quarters of a million?

3. A sports ground holds 32 085 spectators. There are 18 786 seats. How many spectators have to stand when the ground is full?

4. To build one set of steps takes 276 bricks. There are 37 sets of steps to build. How many bricks are needed altogether?

5. Envelopes are sold in packs of 15.
   a How many packs can be made up from 12 650 envelopes?
   b How many envelopes will be left over?

6. There are 48 bags of crisps in a box. A shop sells 20 000 bags of crisps a week.
   a How many full boxes a week is this?
   b How many boxes a year (52 weeks) is this?

7. Subtract nine hundred thousand and two from one and a quarter million.

8. A printer used 6 million sheets of paper to print copies of a new book. Each book used 416 sheets. How many complete books did he print?

9. *Jetair* carry 356 passengers on each flight. In 1996, *Jetair* carried 4 million passengers. How many flights did *Jetair* make in 1996?

10. A humming bird's wings beat 72 times each second. At this rate, after how long will the bird have made half a million wing beats?

Homework N3

1. Which of these are prime numbers?

   9, 2, 13, 15, 11, 23, 24, 25, 142

2. Find the total of the first eight prime numbers.

3. List all the prime numbers that are: greater than 40 and less than 75.

4. Asif gives this clue to his house number:
   add two prime numbers in the thirties

   At what number does Asif live?

5. List the first six multiples of 7.

6. List the first five multiples of 18.

7. A number is: • between 20 and 30
                 • a multiple of 3 and 4.
   What is this number?

8. Which of these are multiples of 6?

   15, 20, 18, 25, 3, 48, 46

9. Is 108 954 a multiple of 9? Explain how you decided.

10. Add the 6th multiple of 18 to the 4th multiple of 19. What multiple of 4 is your answer?

11. List all the factors of 18.

12 List all the factors of 48.

13 Which factors of 24 are also factors of 64?

14 Which factors of 42 are prime numbers?

15 Which prime numbers are factors of 52?

16 List the prime factors of 12.

17 List the prime factors of 200.

18 Give a number that is prime and is also a multiple of 2.

19 Are all multiples of 6 also multiples of 3? Explain.

20 Which numbers less than 40 can be made by adding two or more different prime numbers? List the numbers showing how you made them.

Homework N4

1 Round these numbers to the nearest 10.

   a 37   b 62   c 75
   d 88   e 7   f 41
   g 3   h 188   i 454
   j 865   k 1058   l 833

2 Round these numbers to the nearest 100.

   a 256   b 188   c 231
   d 545   e 862   f 226
   g 153   h 1065   i 1252
   j 6958   k 1962   l 2040

3 Round these numbers to the nearest 1000.

   a 1682   b 2696   c 1388
   d 5629   e 12616   f 10099
   g 10672   h 120602   i 16676

4 A cyclist gave the number of miles travelled in a day as 60, to the nearest 10.

   a What could be the largest number of miles?
   b What could be the shortest distance?

5 To the nearest 100, the number of people on a train was given as 1300.

   Give the smallest number of people that could have been counted.

6 To the nearest ten, the number of sweets in a jar is given as 170.
   Give the smallest number of sweets possible.

7 The number of people at a hockey match was given as 23 600, to the nearest 100.

   What is the largest number of people that could have been at the match?

8 A firm recycles 90 000 cans each week. This number is given to the nearest 1000.

   a What is the smallest number of cans that might be recycled each week?
   b What is the most that might be recycled?

9 The total number of visitors to a beach in a year is given as 170 000, to the nearest 10 000.

   a What could be the largest total?
   b What could be the smallest total?

10 *The Real Pizza Co.* puts 8 olives on a pizza. Jars of olives hold 450, to the nearest ten.

    With one jar of olives, how many pizzas can they be sure of having enough olives for?

11 To the nearest 100 000 tons, India is said to produce 13 million tons of sugar cane.

    Producing how many tons will allow them to claim that 13 500 000 tons are produced?

Homework N5

Do not use a calculator for this homework

1 Round to estimate an answer to each of these.

   a 146 + 182   b 282 - 47
   c 98 - 44   d 154 - 78
   e 196 - 138   f 208 + 395
   g 118 + 24 - 31   h 52 + 75 - 28
   i 225 - 34 + 58   j 1003 - 796 + 88

2 Give an estimate for each of these answers.

   a 12 x 23   b 15 x 38
   c 13 x 27   d 44 x 103
   e 83 ÷ 18   f 157 ÷ 25
   g 148 ÷ 27   h 606 ÷ 47

3 Joel estimates this answer to be 100.

$$335 - 185 =$$

Has he rounded to the nearest 10, or 100? Explain.

4 Mina runs a market stall.
She buys 58 pairs of trainers at £13 a pair.
Estimate the total cost of the trainers.

5 A bag of *Swirls* weighs 38 grams.
Estimate the total weight of 17 bags of *Swirls*.

6 Dave swims 32 lengths of a pool every day.
Estimate the total number of lengths he swims in 45 days.

7 Dan makes shoe laces from waxed cord.
Each lace is 45 cm long.

Estimate how many laces he can make from a roll of cord 125 metres long.

8 A canoe centre opens for 38 weeks a year.
Each week it takes up to 24 students.

Estimate the total number of students the centre can take in a year.

9 A coach seats 56 passengers.

Estimate the number of coaches needed to take 422 fans to a match.

10 Lisa has a pulse of 74 beats a minute.

Estimate how long it will take for her pulse to beat 555 times.

HOMEWORK N6

Do not use a calculator for this homework

1 Make three copies of: $3 + 5 \times 4 - 2 =$
Put in brackets to give an answer of:

   a 30   **b** 21   **c** 16

2 Copy and complete each of these.

   a $3 \times (9 - 6) =$ **b** $35 \div (7 - 2) =$
   c $24 \div (11 - 4 + 1) =$ **d** $(8 - 1) \times (5 + 1) =$
   e $(12 - 4) \div (9 - 7) =$ **f** $(15 - 6) \times 4 \div 12 =$

3 Copy and complete using BODMAS rules:

   a $4 \times 5 - 8 =$ **b** $42 \div 3 + 5 =$
   c $44 - 6 \times 3 =$ **d** $3 \times 18 + 55 =$
   e $9 + 2 \times 5 - 11 =$ **f** $(18 - 14) \times 6 \div 3 =$
   g $(3 + 4) \times (4 - 3) =$ **h** $(15 - 7) \times (2 + 7) =$
   i $14 \times (15 - 7 - 4) =$ **j** $(18 - 9) \div (8 - 5) =$

4 Ian gives the answer to $62 - 4 \times 3$ as 174.
Karen says he is wrong.

Explain who you think is correct, and why.

5 Copy and complete:

$$16 \div 8 + 2 \times 5 - 21 \div 7 =$$

6 The numbers in this calculation are covered.

$$(\blacksquare - \blacksquare) \times (\blacksquare + \blacksquare) = 36$$

Replace each ■ with a number to give an answer of 36.

7 The numbers in this calculation are covered.

$$(\blacksquare + \blacksquare) \div (\blacksquare - \blacksquare) = 8$$

Copy the calculation three times.
Replace each ■ with a number to make three different calculations with an answer of 8.

8 With the numbers 3, 8 and 528,
use one ÷ sign and one + sign to write:

   a a calculation with an answer of 69
   b a calculation with an answer of 48.

9 Find the value of:

   a $25 - 3^2$ **b** $50 - 2^5$ **c** 5^4
   d $3^5 + 3^2$ **e** $7^2 - 1$ **f** 10^6

10 Copy and complete each of these.

   a $(3^2 + 1) \times 7 =$ **b** $(2^3 - 3) \times 15 =$
   c $(2^2 + 3^2) \times 5 =$ **d** $(4^2 - 2^2) \times 3 =$
   e $3^2 + 4^2 - 5^2 =$

HOMEWORK N7

1 List these numbers in order.
Start with the smallest

   6.4   6.15   6.04   6.095   6.0004

2   In the number 15.342, give the value of:

   a the digit 4   **b** the digit 2.

3   Which is larger, 1027.08 or 1027.8?
    Explain.

4   Copy the number: 12.333
    Circle the digit that has a value of $3/100$.

5   Write a three-digit number where one digit has a value of $4/10$.

6   Write a decimal number that is:
    larger than 2.5 but smaller than 2.6

7   Write two numbers that are:
    smaller than 2.04 but larger than 2.03

8   What number is $6/100$ larger than 1.082?

9   What number is $7/10$ less than 5.45?

10 What number is $1/1000$ less than 12.35?

11 Here are some clues to a number.

    • it has two digits and a zero
    • it is less than 1
    • one of the digits has a value of $3/100$
    • one of the digits has a value of $7/10$

    Write down the number.

12 Use a starting number $S = 23.62$

    a Write the number that is $7/10$ more than S.
    b Write the number that is $3/100$ more than S.
    c What number is $1/100$ more than S?

13 Use a starting number $N = 0.4$

    a What number is 10 times larger than N?
    b What number is 100 times larger than N?
    c What number is 1000 times larger than N?
    d What number is 10 times smaller than N?

14 Use all the digits 0, 5, 4 and 3 with a decimal point to make numbers.

    a What is the smallest number you can make?
    b What is the largest number you can make?
    c What is the largest number you can make that is less than 1?

HOMEWORK N8

Do not use a calculator for this homework

1   Copy and complete these calculations.

    a 12.4 + 26.52 + 1.7 =
    b 1.06 + 0.3 + 5.07 + 16 =
    c 46.62 + 3.005 + 153.8 =
    d 0.4 + 0.054 + 0.0003 =
    e 1000.14 + 1.04 + 14.001 =

2   Copy and complete these calculations.

    a 125.2 - 19.6 =
    b 88.05 - 39.6 =
    c 250 - 117.86 =
    d 5 - 0.006 =
    e 0.45 - 0.045 =

3   Give the next 3 numbers in each pattern.

    a 1, 1.55, 2.1, 2.65, ...
    b 0, 0.04, 0.08, ...
    c 12, 10.75, 9.5, 8.25, ...
    d 1, 0.965, 0.93, 0.895, ...

4   What number is 0.4 less than one thousand?

5   What number is 4.04 less than one million?

6   Gary wants to know what his dog weighs.
    He uses bathroom scales with these results.

    Gary on his own weighs 82.2 kg
    Gary and the dog together weigh 95.24 kg

    Find how much the dog weighs.

7   A small trailer can carry no more than 295 kg.
    Jenny can make one trip with the trailer and has these boxes to move.

    | Box A weighs | 102.81 kg |
    | Box B weighs | 98.38 kg |
    | Box C weighs | 102.62 kg |
    | Box D weighs | 93.85 kg |

    Which boxes can she take in one trip?
    Explain.

8   Jan and Gita both throw the javelin.
    Jan threw 62.96 metres and Gita 63.04 metres.

    Who threw further, and by how much?

HOMEWORK N9

Do not use a calculator for this homework

1 Copy and complete:

   a 6.57 × 4 =   b 35.08 × 7 =
   c 25.165 × 9 =   d 186.75 × 4 =
   e 465.108 × 6 =   f 2.34 × 12 =
   g 378.65 × 3 =   h 0.086 × 5 =
   i 0.00564 × 9 =   j 0.00097 × 8 =

2 Copy and complete:

   a 49.2 ÷ 3 =   b 110.4 ÷ 4 =
   c 21.56 ÷ 7 =   d 24.102 ÷ 6 =
   e 488.43 ÷ 9 =   f 832.56 ÷ 8 =
   g 0.87 ÷ 6 =   h 0.2352 ÷ 4 =
   i 0.0001 ÷ 2 =   j 0.001503 ÷ 3 =

3 Copy and complete:

   a 1.56 × 3 ÷ 2 =   b 0.85 × 4 ÷ 5 =

4 A piece of wood 2.4 metres long is cut into three pieces of equal length.
   How long is each piece?

5 A portable TV weighs 4.58 kg.
   Calculate the total weight of seven of these.

6 A 3.5 kg bag of chips gives 8 equal servings.
   Calculate how much each serving weighs.

7 The weight of one pencil is 15.08 grams.
   Calculate the total weight of:

   a 9 pencils   b 5 pencils
   c 10 pencils   d 55 pencils

8 A total of 0.3872 tonnes of milk powder is packed equally into 8 crates.
   How much milk powder is in each crate?

HOMEWORK N10

1 Round these numbers to 1 dp.

   a 6.54   b 12.61   c 56.06
   d 12.54   e 157.15   f 100.09
   g 1.909   h 0.08   i 1.99
   j 2.95   k 0.882   l 45.05
   m 0.15   n 0.056   o 599.48

2 Round these to 2 dp.

   a 12.616   b 34.085   c 0.072
   d 100.088   e 31.135   f 9.765
   g 12.096   h 121.537 i 2.296

3 Which of these become 15.5 when you round to 1 dp?
   a 15.47   b 15.546   c 15.05

4 Lenny rounds a 3-digit number to 2.7
   Before rounding, what could have been:
   a the largest number?
   b the smallest number?

5 What is the smallest 4-digit number that, when rounded to 2 dp, becomes 3.12?

6 a Without a calculator, work out: 53.62 × 4
   b Round your answer to 1 dp.

Do not use a calculator for questions 7 to 10

7 Copy and complete:

   a 1.23 × 10 =   b 34.102 × 100 =
   c 0.0544 × 100 =   d 1.1055 × 1000 =
   e 147.081 × 100 =   f 0.0564 × 20 =
   g 0.00152 × 60 000 =   h 1.0825 × 400 =
   i 0.1 × 8 000 =   j 1.4 × 3 000 000 =

8 Copy and complete:

   a 158.4 ÷ 10 =   b 246.5 ÷ 100 =
   c 12.5 ÷ 1000 =   d 34.2 ÷ 200 =
   e 0.54 ÷ 10 =   f 1.25 ÷ 5000 =
   g 0.3 ÷ 10 000 =   h 0.04 ÷ 100 =
   i 65 ÷ 5000 =   j 10.1 ÷ 200 000 =

9 Copy and complete: 12.435 × 300 =

10 Copy and complete: 583.14 ÷ 200 =

HOMEWORK N11

Do not use a calculator for this homework

1 Calculate the total cost of these items.

   apples £1.06, crisps 72p, cola 35p

2 Pencils cost 23p.
   With £3, what is the largest number of pencils you can buy? Explain.

3 Rose trees are advertised in this way.

> **Rose Trees** for sale at £3.85 each.
> Spend £10 or more and we will
> take £2.50 off your bill.

   a What is the total cost of seven rose trees?
   b What would you pay for 15 rose trees?

4 Emma buys a box of eight batteries for £5.52
   Find the cost of one battery.

5 A single bag of crisps costs 32p.
   A six-bag pack of these crisps costs £1.79
   How much is saved in total buying the pack?

6 Fence posts cost £3.79 each.
   Fencing rails cost £2.32 each.

   a Find the total cost of 5 posts and 8 rails.
   b Find the total cost of this fence.

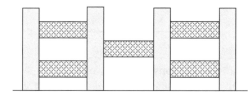

   The fence continues with eight more posts.

   c How many more rails are used?
   d Find the total cost of this longer fence.

7 Nigel makes jeans.
   For each pair, he uses 9 rivets and 5 buttons.
   Rivets cost 3p each.
   Buttons cost 34p each.

   What is the total cost of rivets and buttons
   for 150 pairs of jeans?

8 To process a film with 24 prints:

   Fastprint   charge £5.99
   Bettaprint charge 21p a print
                         plus
                         75p a film

   Which is cheaper, *Fastprint* or *Bettaprint*?
   Explain.

HOMEWORK N12

Do not use a calculator for this homework

1 Copy and complete:

   a 5 - 8 =   **b** 6 - 14 =
   c 14 - 45 =   **d** 3 - 55 =
   e 4 - 100 =   **f** 19 - 44 =
   g 5 - 12 + 3 =   **h** 24 + 3 - 35 =
   i 34 + 16 - 100 =   **j** 12 - 16 - 24 =

2 Copy and complete:

   a $^-4 + 7 =$ **b** $^-6 + 11 =$
   c $^-2 + 21 =$ **d** $^-8 + 5 =$
   e $^-9 + 2 =$ **f** $^-11 + 3 + 6 =$
   g $^-6 + 3 - 5 =$ **h** $^-21 + 6 - 15 =$
   i $^-18 - 4 =$ **j** $^-15 - 35 =$

3 Copy and complete this addition table.

+	14	6	$^-2$	3	$^-8$	0	$^-1$	1	$^-5$
$^-3$				$^-5$				$^-2$	
$^-15$									
$^-22$						$^-23$			

4 Copy and complete:

   a $5 - ^-4 =$ **b** $6 - ^-5 =$
   c $^-2 - ^-7 =$ **d** $^-8 - ^-1 =$
   e $5 - 7 - ^-2 =$ **f** $^-6 - 4 - ^-12 =$
   g $^-22 - 4 - ^-17 =$ **h** $2 - 15 - ^-3 - 1 =$
   i $^-12 - 5 + 1 - ^-8 =$ **j** $^-55 - 18 - ^-3 =$

5 Copy and complete this subtraction table.

Second number

First number −	12	7	$^-5$	3	$^-6$	0	$^-9$	1	$^-4$
$^-2$				3				$^-3$	
$^-17$									
$^-21$					$^-24$				

6 Frozen chickens are stored at $^-18\,°C$.
   A chicken is thawed to a room temperature
   of $19\,°C$.
   How many degrees did it rise in temperature?

7 Jade added two numbers from this list and made an answer of ⁻8.

3, ⁻4, ⁻3, ⁻1, 8, ⁻5, 4, 7

Which two numbers did she add?

8 Dave took part in the *Great Trivia Final*.
He won 20 points for each correct answer, but he lost 50 points for each wrong answer.

This was Dave's score-sheet.

Contestant	Dave
Correct answers	18
Wrong answers	13

What was Dave's points score in the final?

HOMEWORK N13

1 For each shape, what fraction is shaded?

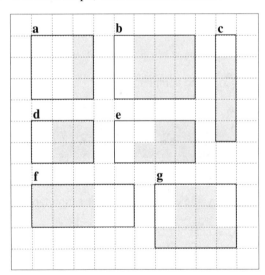

2 Copy this shape and shade ⁵/₈ of it.

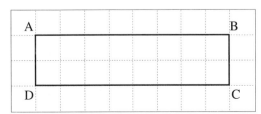

3 Make three copies of shape CDEF.

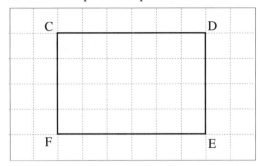

  a On one copy, shade ³/₈ of the shape.
  b On one copy, shade ⁵/₆ of the shape.
  c On one copy, shade ⁷/₁₂ of the shape.

4 Make two copies of shape RSTV.

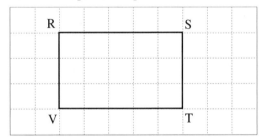

  a On one copy, shade ²/₃ of RSTV.
  b On the other copy, shade ³/₅ of RSTV.
  c Which is larger: ³/₅ or ²/₃ ? Explain.

5 Make 4 copies of shape KLMN.

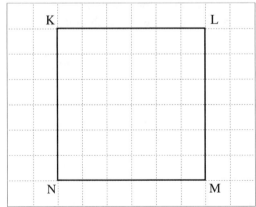

  a On one copy each, shade these fractions:

⁷/₁₂ , ²/₃ , ⁵/₉ , ³/₄

  b Which fraction is the largest?
  c List the fractions in order.
    Start with the smallest

HOMEWORK N14

Do not use a calculator for this homework

1. Find:
   a. $1/5$ of 20 pencils
   b. $3/5$ of 25 pencils
   c. $2/3$ of 27 pens
   d. $5/8$ of 40 cars
   e. $7/10$ of 120 cans
   f. $7/10$ of 250 cards.

2. In a survey of 80 cars:
   $1/4$ of the cars were red,
   $2/5$ of the cars were white,
   $3/10$ of the cars were blue,
   the rest were *other colours*.

   a. How many cars were red?
   b. How many cars were white?
   c. How many cars were blue?
   d. How many cars were *other colours*?
   e. What fraction were *other colours*?

3. *Fastflame* sell three sizes of cola can:
   Regular, Large, and Mega

   On one day, they sold 360 cans altogether.
   $2/9$ were Regular cans,
   $5/12$ were Large,
   the rest were Mega.

   a. How many cans of each size were sold?
   b. What fraction of the cans sold were Mega?

4. Five friends share six pizzas between them.
   They all have an equal share.
   How much pizza is each person's share?

5. In a case of 60 tins of cat food:
   $2/5$ of the tins are sardine,
   $4/15$ of the tins are cereal,
   $1/12$ are beef,
   $1/10$ are chicken,
   and the rest are turkey.

   a. How many tins are there of each variety?
   b. What fraction are turkey variety?
   c. Joel buys three cases of cat food.
      What fraction of these tins are cereal?

6. A *tug-of-war* team (8 people) share a prize of three fruit cakes equally between them.
   What is each person's share?

7. In a box of 45 chocolates:
   $4/9$ are milk chocolate,
   $2/5$ are plain chocolate,
   the rest are white chocolate.

   a. How many are white chocolate?
      Explain your reasons.
   b. What fraction are white chocolate?

HOMEWORK N15

1. Make a copy of these shapes.

   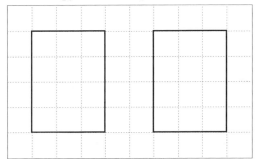

   a. Shade $3/4$ of one shape.
   b. Shade $9/12$ of the other shape.
   c. Explain why $3/4$ and $9/12$ are equivalent fractions.
   d. Give two other fractions equivalent to $3/4$.

2. Which of these is **not** equivalent to $3/8$?

   $30/80$, $36/96$, $21/56$, $300/8000$

3. Which of these are equivalent to $3/5$?

   $16/25$, $24/45$, $24/40$, $51/85$

4. Which is larger: $4/6$ or $2/3$?
   Explain your answer with a diagram.

5. Twenty runners shared 16 oranges equally.
   Which of these statements is true?
   Explain your answers with diagrams.
   a. Each runner had $4/5$ of an orange.
   b. Each runner had more than $1/2$.
   c. Each runner had less than $3/4$.
   d. Each runner had less than $7/10$.

6 Write each of these in its lowest terms.

  a $8/10$ **b** $12/30$ **c** $15/40$
  d $24/32$ **e** $33/121$ **f** $36/63$
  g $75/175$ **h** $11/15$ **i** $27/48$

7 Which is smaller: $450/750$ or $44/55$? Explain.

8 Write each of these as a mixed number.

  a $17/4$ **b** $25/8$ **c** $11/3$
  d $36/5$ **e** $45/7$ **f** $19/2$

HOMEWORK N16

1 Write each ratio in its lowest terms.

  a 5 : 20   **b** 12 : 18   **c** 24 : 32
  d 21 : 35 **e** 45 : 27   **f** 175 : 75

2 Which of these are equivalent ratios?

  15 : 40   30 : 75   21 : 56   7 : 20

3 In a group the ratio of boys to girls is 3 : 5.

  a What fraction of the group is girls?
  b What fraction of the group is boys?

4 In 1999 a team won $2/5$ of the games played.

  Give the ratio, win : not win, for the team.

5 A club has 40 players.
  25 of the players have never scored a goal.

  a What fraction of the players are goal scorers?
  b Give the ratio, scorers : non scorers, in its lowest terms.

6 Divide each amount in the ratio given.

	Divide	in the ratio
a	60 kg	5 : 7
b	125 km	12 : 13
c	72 miles	3 : 5
d	342 hours	5 : 4
e	204 mm	11 : 6

7 £400 is shared between Ed and Shelley in the ratio 2 : 3.
  How much does each receive?

8 Nina and Anik share a sum of money in the ratio 7 : 5. Anik's share is £355.

  a How much in total do they share?
  b What is Nina's share of the total?

9 A recipe for 24 biscuits uses 216 g of flour. How much flour is needed for 40 biscuits?

10 In 80 litres of compost there are 6.5 litres of sand. How much sand is used to make one million litres of compost?

11 To make 320 litres of cola 28 g of colouring is used. With 3.5 kg of colouring how much cola can be produced?

HOMEWORK N17

1 Copy and complete this table.

Fraction	Percentage
	25%
	75%
	10%
	50%
	20%
	80%

2 Copy and complete this table.

Decimal	Percentage
	65%
	48%
	16%
	27%
	6%
	12.5%

3 Convert these fractions to decimals.

  a $12/100$ **b** $56/100$ **c** $3/100$
  d $74/100$ **e** $81/100$ **f** $7/100$
  g $36/200$ **h** $15/300$ **i** $4/400$

4 Convert each decimal to a fraction in its lowest terms, and to a percentage.

  a 0.45   **b** 0.18   **c** 0.04   **d** 0.09

5 Convert each percentage to a fraction in its lowest terms, and to a ~~percentage~~ decimal.

a 65%	b 24%	c 15%	d 8%
e 40%	f 32%	g 30%	h 2%
i 5%	j 98%	k 36%	l 7%

6 25%, $\frac{1}{4}$, and 0.25 are all equivalent.
Give a fraction and a decimal equivalent to each of these.

a 6% b 7.5% c 1.5% d 4.25%

7 A group of people won a prize.

> Jenny's share was 12% of the prize
> Bryn's share was 0.14 of the prize
> Marie's share was $\frac{3}{20}$ of the prize

Who had the largest share?
Explain.

8 About 72% of the Earth's surface is water.
Roughly what percentage is land?

9 Emil works out that he spends 12.5% of his time watching TV.
What percentage of his time is spent **not** watching TV?

HOMEWORK N18

1 A hockey club has 472 members.

> 50% of the members are female
> 25% of the members are students
> 75% of the members voted for the captain

a How many of the members are students?
b How many members voted for the captain?
c Are more than 235 of the members female? Explain.

2 *H-Preserves* make 3400 jars of jam a week.
Of these jars, 75% hold strawberry jam.

a How many jars hold strawberry jam?
b How many do **not** hold strawberry jam?

3 Carl checked 5450 batteries and found that 10% of them had faults.
a How many batteries had faults?
b How many did **not** have faults?

4 A school has 660 pupils. Of these, 20% are in Year 7, and 25% are in Year 8.

a How many pupils are in Year 7?
b How many pupils are in Year 8?

5 Read this newspaper cutting.

14   Northern Chronicle

More cyclists hurt last year

Last year there were 1680 accidents and 30% of them involved cyclists.

a How many accidents involved cyclists?
b What percentage did **not** involve cyclists?
c How many did **not** involve cyclists?

6 In a traffic survey, Jan counted 3680 cars leaving the motorway.
Of these, 80% carried only the driver.

How many cars carried more than the driver?

7 On one day a museum had 1396 visitors.
Of these visitors, 75% were adults.

a What percentage were **not** adults?
b How many of the visitors were adults?

8 An aircraft carried 340 passengers to Spain.
Of the passengers, 90% were going on holiday.

How many passengers were going on holiday?

9 *Clearspring* produce 6 million bottles of sparkling water each year.
30% of these are peach flavour and 40% are apple flavour.

a How many bottles are peach flavour?
b How many are apple flavour?

10 An athletics stadium holds 45 500 spectators.
Of all the tickets sold, 70% are for seats and 30% are for standing.

a How many seat tickets can be sold?
b How many standing tickets can be sold?
c 20% of the seat tickets can be reserved. How many tickets is this?

Algebra

Homework A1

1 Draw the next three patterns in this sequence.

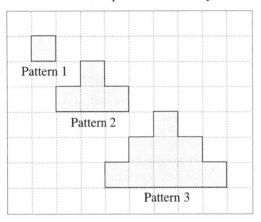

2 For each sequence, give the next three terms.

   a 1, 3, 5, 7, ...
   b 7, 14, 21, 28, ...
   c 2, 4, 8, 16, ...
   d 80, 40, 20, ...
   e 1, 6, 16, 31, ...

3 For each sequence, give the next three terms.

   a $\frac{1}{2}$, $\frac{1}{4}$, $\frac{1}{8}$, ...
   b 2.5, 2.25, 2, ...
   c 0.35, 0.7, 1.05, ...
   d 1, 1.5, 2.5, 4.5, ...
   e 0.6, 1.2, 1.8, 3, ...

4 This is the start of the sequence of square numbers.

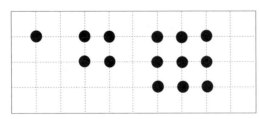

   a What is the fifth square number?
   b List the first fifteen square numbers.
   c Is 360 a square number?
      Explain how you decided.

5 List all the square numbers that are greater than 400 and less than 600.

6 A virus doubles its number of cells every hour. If the virus starts with a single cell, how many cells will there be after 24 hours?

7 This is the start of the sequence of triangle numbers.

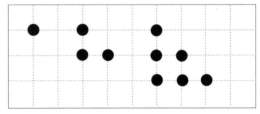

   a List the first six triangle numbers.
   b Is 91 a triangle number?
      Explain how you decided.

8 The rule for the next term in a sequence is:

   add 3

   The sequence starts in this way:

   2, 5, ...

   a Copy and continue the sequence for the first six terms.
   b Is 47 a term in this sequence?
      Explain how you decided.

9 Write a rule for the next term in this sequence.

   1, 5, 9, 13, ...

10 Write a rule for the next term in this sequence.

   8, 2, ⁻4, ⁻10, ...

Homework A2

1 Copy and complete this number machine.

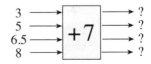

2 Copy and complete this number machine.

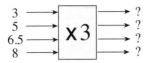

3 Copy and complete this table for the number machines below.

Machine	Rule
a	+5
b	
c	
d	
e	
f	

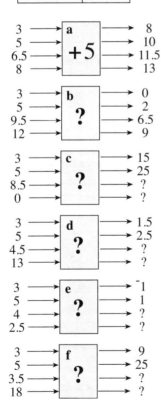

4 Copy and complete number machines **c**, **d**, **e**, and **f** in question **3**.

5 Copy and complete these number machines.

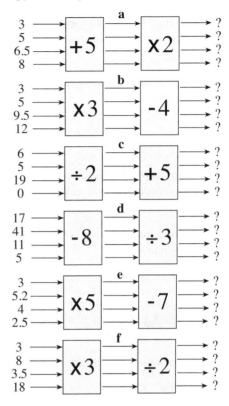

6 Give a rule for each of these number machines.

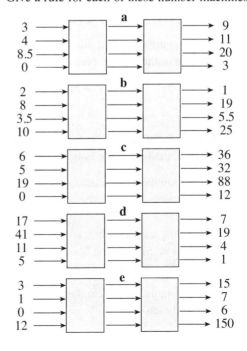

15

HOMEWORK A3

1. The total cost, C, of processing a film is worked out by adding the developing cost, d, to the printing cost, p.

   Write a formula for processing a film, that begins:

   $C = $ ....

2. The total cost, T, of a can of lemonade is worked out by adding:
   - the cost of the can, c
   - the cost of the lemonade, l
   - and the profit, p

   Write a formula for the total cost of a can of lemonade, that begins:

   $T = $ ....

3. Ciara is walking 500 miles for charity. On the first day, she walked w miles, leaving her a distance of d miles still to walk.

   Write a formula for the distance, that begins:

   $d = $ ....

4. Jill plants 25 cabbage plants in each row.

   Write a formula for the total number of cabbage plants, t, when she plants r rows.

5. The total charge T for an item from a catalogue is the cost of the item, c, plus £4.55 postage.

   Write a formula for the charge, £T.

   $T = $ ....

6. The cost of a holiday, C, is £450 minus the deposit, d, paid when the holiday was booked.

   Write a formula for the amount to pay, £P.

   $P = $ ....

7. On a cycling holiday, Emma travelled a total of 748 miles. She was on holiday for n days, and each day she cycled the same distance.

   Write a formula for the number of miles, m, she cycled each day.

   $m = $ ....

8. A lottery prize of £8.8 million is shared equally between w winners. Each winner wins a prize, £p.

   Write a formula for each winner's prize.

   $p = $ ....

9. The price of a bike, £p, is reduced in a sale by £35.

   Write a formula for the sale price, £s.

   $s = $ ....

10. Bracelets are made from gold chain. The chain comes on reels of 100 metres. From each reel, n necklaces are made. Each necklace is l centimetres long.

    Write a formula for l.

    $l = $ ....

HOMEWORK A4

1. *Seaferry* use this formula to calculate the charge, £C, for each car.

   $C = 8.50 \times l$ where l is the length of the car in metres.

   Copy the table below, and use the formula to work out the charge for each car.

Car	Length (metres)	Charge (£)
K334 TRV	4	
F188 WRS	5.5	
G671 TVD	4.2	
L434 YAD	4.6	
M341 KJL	4.9	

2. Use the formula $d = 475 - n$ to calculate:

   a. the value of d when $n = 156.65$
   b. the value of d when $n = 0.085$
   c. the value of d when $n = 13.03$
   d. the value of n when $d = 134$

3 This is a formula for the price, £P, of an item in a shop.

$P = c + v$ where c is the cost in £s and v is the VAT in £s.

Use the formula to calculate:
a the value of P when $c = 44.2$ and $v = 7.74$
b the value of P when $c = 7.99$ and $v = 1.40$
c the value of c when $P = 33.37$ and $v = 4.97$

4 A group of n people play the lottery and share any prize win w equally. Each player gets £p.

a Write a formula that begins: $p = $ ....

Use your formula to calculate:
b the value of p when: $w = £6.5$ million and $n = 4$
c the value of p when: $w = £22.3$ million and $n = 14$
d the value of n when: $w = £15.4$ million and $p = 1\,925\,000$

5 Use the formula $w = (2 \times t) + 6.55$ to calculate:

a the value of w when $t = 13.5$
b the value of w when $t = 0.04$
c the value of w when $t = 15$ million
d the value of t when $w = 67.55$
e the value of t when $w = 30.63$

6 Use the formula $g = (v - t) \times 4.5$ to calculate:

a the value of g when $v = 14$ and $t = 9$
b the value of g when $v = 25.4$ and $t = 16.9$
c the value of g when $v = 3.04$ and $t = 0$
d the value of v when $g = 18$ and $t = 5$
e the value of v when $g = 0$ and $t = 0.04$

7 Use the formula $k = (a \times b) - 12.5$ to calculate:

a the value of k when $a = 4$ and $b = 7$
b the value of k when $a = 3.5$ and $b = 6.5$
c the value of k when $a = 0$ and $b = 20$
d the value of a when $k = 17.5$ and $b = 15$
e the value of a when $k = 0$ and $b = 62.5$

8 Using the formula $n = (a + b - c) \times 2$

a find n when $a = 3.5$, $b = 8.5$, and $c = 7.5$
b find n when $a = 14$, $b = 8.2$, and $c = 17.6$
c find c when $n = 4$, $a = 16$, and $b = 12.5$

HOMEWORK A5

1 Collect like terms in each of these expressions.

a $k + k + k + k$ b $n + n + n + n$
c $3y + 2y + 4y$ d $5h - 3h$
e $9g - g$ f $6y + 4y - 2y$
g $5h - h + 3h$ h $4d - 9d + 5d$
i $8p + p - 9p + p$ j $5m + 3m - m$

2 Collect like terms in each of these expressions.

a $3y + 5v - 2y$ b $k + 6d + 3k - d$
c $4h + 3 + 7h$ d $9n + 5r - n + 2r$
e $6y + 3a - y + a$ f $3b + g + 2b - 4$
g $a + 2b - 3c + 4a$ h $8d - a + 3d - a$
i $4h + 3n - h + 2n$ j $3a + 2 - a - 5$

3 Rewrite each of these expressions showing the hidden terms.

a $4y + ■ - 5a - ■ = 3y - 5a + 3$
b $7n + ■ - ■ + a - ■ = 6n - 2a + 3$
c $■ - 3k + y + ■ - 8 + ■ = 7y - 3$

4 When like terms were collected in each of the expressions below, the answer was:

$$3k + 5c - 1$$

Rewrite each of these expressions showing the hidden terms.

a $2k + ■ + 4c + ■ - ■$
b $c - ■ + 8k + ■ - ■$
c $4 + 3k - ■ + 6c - ■$
d $k - ■ + c + ■ + ■$
e $8c - ■ - ■ + c + ■$
f $4k + c - ■ + ■ - ■$

5 Collect like terms in each of these expressions.

a $g - 8 + 3g - 5v + 4 + 12v - g - 1$
b $7y + y + 4 - 8y - 4a - a - 4 - 5a$
c $n - a - n - a + 3 + 5n + 4 + 4a$
d $5b - 4 - 5b - 4$

6 Collect like terms in each of these.

a $y + y - 1 + y - 2 + 5 - 3y$
b $g - 5t + g - 4 - 2g + 5t$
c $5 + 3v - 2a + a - 5v + 1 - a - 2v$
d $11k + 8 - k - 10 - k + 18 - 8k$

17

Homework A6

1 If $p = 3$, $k = 4$, and $g = 5$, give the value of:

- **a** $3p$
- **b** $25k$
- **c** $g - k$
- **d** $5k - 8$
- **e** $20 - 6p$
- **f** $8g - 7p$
- **g** $65p + k$
- **h** $2k + 3g$
- **i** $5p - 3g$
- **j** $p + k - g$
- **k** $5p + 4k - g$
- **l** $7g - 9k + 3p$
- **m** $100k - 25g - 75p$
- **n** $5p + 5k - 7g$
- **o** $1.5k + 2.5g$
- **p** $\frac{1}{2}k + \frac{1}{3}p$
- **q** $\frac{3}{5}g + \frac{2}{3}p$

2 Give the value of each expression when:

$w = 2$, $y = 5$, and $t = 8$

- **a** $w + y$
- **b** $2t - 3y$
- **c** $y - \frac{1}{2}w$
- **d** $3y - 4$
- **e** $3y - t - 4w$
- **f** wy
- **g** $wt - t$
- **h** $150 - ty$
- **i** $3w + yw - t$
- **j** $yw + ty - tw$
- **k** $2y + yt - 18$
- **l** $wt - y + 1$
- **m** $yw - t - 10$
- **n** $tw - 2yw$

3 Give the value of each expression when:

$p = 3$, $r = 7$, and $u = 4$

- **a** p^2
- **b** r^2
- **c** u^2
- **d** $u^2 - 5$
- **e** $p^2 + 2p$
- **f** p^3
- **g** $15u - r^2$
- **h** $p^2 - 2p$
- **i** pru
- **j** $5r - u^2$
- **k** $ru - pr$
- **l** $\frac{1}{2}r^2$

4 The values of k, n, p, and w are:

$k = 5$, $n = 12$, $p = 6$, and $w = 21$

Copy and complete these expressions.

- **a** $kn - \blacksquare = 39$
- **b** $3n - kp - \blacksquare = 1$
- **c** $n^2 + \blacksquare - w = 133$
- **d** $pw - \blacksquare = 101$
- **e** $3w + \blacksquare - kn = 75$
- **f** $\blacksquare + \blacksquare = 180$
- **g** $kp - w + \blacksquare + \blacksquare = 36$
- **h** $pw - \blacksquare + kn = 146$
- **i** $9p + \blacksquare + k^2 = 175$

5 a If $v^2 = 64$, what is the value of v?
  b If $0.5k = 13$, what is the value of k?
  c If $\frac{3}{5}y = 12$, what is the value of y?
  d If $3w = 1$, what is the value of w?

Homework A7

1 Copy these axes.

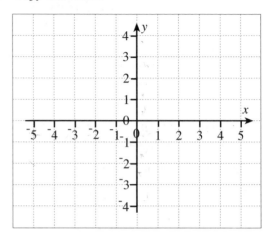

a On your axes, draw and label each of these lines:

$x = 2$ $\quad y = {}^-3$
$x = {}^-4$ $\quad y = 1$

b On your axes, draw and label the line $y = x$.

2 List the co-ordinates of 4 points on your line $x = 2$.

3 List the co-ordinates of 4 points on your line $y = {}^-3$.

4 List the co-ordinates of three points that will be on the line $x = 8$.

5 List the co-ordinates of three points that will be on the line $y = {}^-6$.

6 Will the point (12, 12) be on the line $y = x$? Explain.

7 Give the co-ordinates of the point where the lines $x = 2$ and $y = {}^-3$ cross each other.

8 Give the co-ordinates of the point where the lines $x = {}^-4$ and $y = 1$ cross.

9 Give the co-ordinates of the point where the line $x = 5$ and the line $y = 2$ cross.

10 Is the x-axis the line $x = 0$, or the line $y = 0$? Explain.

11 Copy and complete this pattern for $y = x + 1$.

```
x  --+1-->  y
-2  ------>  -1
-1  ------>   0
 0  ------>   ?
 1  ------>   ?
 2  ------>   ?
 3  ------>   ?
 4  ------>   ?
```

12 Copy and complete this set of co-ordinates for the line $y = x + 1$.

(-2, ?) (-1, ?) (0, ?) (1, ?)

(2, ?) (3, ?) (4, ?)

13 a Copy the axes from question 1.
    b On your axes, draw the graph of $y = x + 1$.

14 Copy and complete these co-ordinates of points on the line $y = 2x + 1$.

(6, ?) (-5, ?) (12, ?) (15, ?) (21, ?)

15 Which of these points are on the line $y = x$?

(2, 1) (3, 3) (-1, -1) (4, 5) (7, 7)

Explain.

16 Copy and complete these co-ordinates, of points on the line $y = 3x + 4$.

(-5, ?) (-4, ?) (-1, ?) (0, ?) (3, ?)

17 Copy and complete these co-ordinates of points on the line $y = 4x - 3$.

(-3, ?) (-2, ?) (0, ?) (1, ?) (3, ?)

18 Which of these points are on the line $y = x - 1$?

(-1, 1) (0, 1) (0, -1) (2, 2) (2, 1)

19 Which of these points is on both of the lines $y = x$ and $x = 3$?

(2, 3) (3, 4) (4, 3) (3, 3)

20 a Which of these points are on the line $y = -4$?

(1, 0) (1, -4) (4, 4) (-4, 1) (5, -4)

   b Which of these points are on the line $x = 8$?

(1, 8) (8, 1) (0, 8) (8, 0) (2, 8)

HOMEWORK A8

1 Solve these equations.

a $5y = 60$ b $3k = 24$
c $4w = 28$ d $4p = 280$
e $9a = 225$ f $14t = 196$
g $\frac{1}{2} b = 9$ h $\frac{1}{4} n = 15$

2 Solve these equations.

a $y + 3 = 11$ b $k + 4 = 22$
c $4 + w = 25$ d $p + 23 = 30$
e $a - 35 = 50$ f $t + 1 = 99$
g $b - 125 = 200$ h $n + 1 = 1$ million
i $4.5 + v = 15$ j $d - 9.2 = 10$
k $h + \frac{1}{2} = 5$ l $y - \frac{3}{4} = 9$

3 Solve these equations.

a $3y + 1 = 13$ b $8k + 5 = 77$
c $4w - 7 = 17$ d $9p - 4 = 77$
e $5a - 18 = 27$ f $14 + 3t = 56$
g $4 + 3b = 40$ h $8n - 32 = 24$
i $24w + 18 = 90$ j $15d - 12 = 68$
k $\frac{1}{2} h + 4 = 16$ l $1.5y - 2 = 10$

4 For each of these statements, write an equation and solve it to find the starting number.

a You have a number, then you add 12. The answer is 21.
b You have a number, then you subtract 7. The answer is 35.
c You have a number, then you double it. The answer is 42.
d You have a number, then you double it. The answer is 15.

5 For each of these statements, write an equation and solve it to find the starting number.

a Start with a number, double it, then add 7. The answer is 39.
b Start with a number, multiply by three, then subtract 5. The answer is 22.
c Start with a number, divide by six, then add 42. The answer is 50.

HOMEWORK A9

1. You can solve the equation $6y - 8 = 46$ by trial and improvement.

   a. Try a first guess, such as $y = 5$.
      Is 5 too big, or too small?
   b. Try a second guess, such as $y = 10$.
      Is 10 too big, or too small?
   c. Try other guesses and solve the equation.

2. Use a table like this to solve the equation $7w - 5 = 44$ by trial and improvement.

Equation	try	Answer	Too big/small
$7w - 5 = 44$	$w = 3$	16	too small

3. Use a trial and improvement table to solve these equations.

   a. $7w + 4 = 60$
   b. $15y + 3 = 108$
   c. $12v - 7 = 89$
   d. $9k - 12 = 150$
   e. $9 + 15h = 204$
   f. $4n + 65 = 285$

4. Use trial and improvement to solve:

   a. $w^2 = 64$
   b. $k^2 = 225$
   c. $h^2 = 529$
   d. $a^2 = 5929$
   e. $v^2 = 282.24$

5. Use trial and improvement to solve:

   $$k^2 + 4 = 217.16$$

HOMEWORK A10

1. Give the inverse of each of these.

   a. *add 43*
   b. *subtract 157*
   c. *multiply by 4.5*
   d. *divide by 8*

2. Write down the inverse of:

   multiply by 4   then   add 3

3. Draw the inverse of each of these number machines.

   a.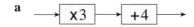

   b. → +8 → ×5 →

   c. → -6 → ÷9 →

   d. → ÷6 → ÷2.5 →

   e. → ×3 → ×0.5 →

   f. → ×1.5 → ×5 →

   g. → +3 → +4.5 →

4. Copy and complete this number machine to solve the equation $5w - 4 = 21$.

   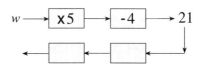

5. Draw a number machine to show how you solve each of these equations.

   a. $6k + 3 = 27$
   b. $12c - 18 = 186$
   c. $8k - 55 = 17$
   d. $7h + 14 = 133$
   e. $17n - 24 = 248$

6. a. What equation is this number machine being used to solve?

   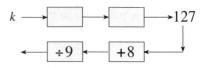

   b. Copy the machine and solve the equation.

7. Draw a number machine to find the starting number.

   Start with a number, multiply by 4, then add 56.
   The answer is 180.

8. Draw a number machine and solve $y^2 = 441$.

Shape, Space and Measures

Homework S1

1 List the co-ordinates of points A to G.

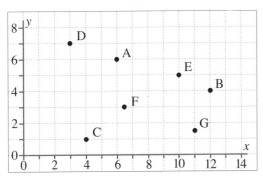

2 Plot and join up these co-ordinates in the order they are given. Use axes between 0 and 14.

(5, 2), (4, 2), (4, 1), (5, 1), (5, 13), (6, 13), (7, 12), (7, 11), (6, 10), (3, 10), (1, 8), (1, 5), (3, 3), (5, 3), (7, 4), (8, 6), (7, 8), (6, 8), (4, 7)

What shape have you drawn?

3 In each case, the co-ordinates of three corners of a rectangle are given.
Give the co-ordinates of the fourth corner.

   a (5, 1), (2, 3), (2, 1)
   b (10, 5), (4, 13), (10, 13)
   c (9, 2), (12, 5), (8, 9)
   d (18, 2), (14, 1), (12, 9)

4 Line AB goes from (4, 12) to (11, 5).
Line CD goes from (1, 7) to (10, 10).
What are the co-ordinates of the point where the two lines cross?

5 A straight line passes through the points (3, 1) and (6, 7).
What are the co-ordinates of the point where the line crosses the x-axis?

6 A line joins (12, 4) to (2, 14).
What are the co-ordinates of its mid-point?

7 On axes from 0 to 8, draw a kite using four points with whole number co-ordinates.
List the co-ordinates you use.

Homework S2

1 Draw x and y axes from ⁻4 to 4.
Plot and label the points: A(3, ⁻2), B(⁻4, 1), C(1, 3), D(⁻2, ⁻3), E(⁻3, 3), F(1, ⁻2).

2 List the co-ordinates of points A to G.

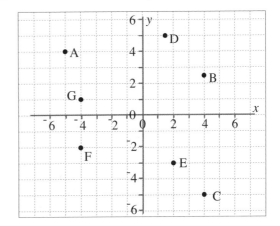

3 A square has corners at (⁻3, 2), (1, 2), (1, ⁻2) and (⁻3, ⁻2). Give the co-ordinates of the centre of the square.

4 Plot and join up these co-ordinates in the order they are given.

(3, ⁻2), (⁻2, ⁻2), (⁻2, 6), (1, 6), (1, 1), (3, 1), (3, ⁻2)

What shape have you drawn?

5 A straight line passes through the points (⁻4, ⁻3) and (2, ⁻3).
At what point does the line cross the y-axis?

6 A straight line starts at (⁻3, 3) and its mid-point is at (⁻1, 2). What are the co-ordinates of the other end of the line?

7 The points (-3, 2), (4, 2), and (-3, -1) are all vertices of the same rectangle.

Give the co-ordinates of the other vertex.

8 A circle passes through these points.
   (⁻1, 4), (2, 1), (⁻1, ⁻2), (⁻4, 1)
Give the co-ordinates of the centre of the circle.

HOMEWORK S3

1 What is the name of a polygon with:

   a 4 sides?   b 5 sides?
   c 6 sides?   d 8 sides?
   e 10 sides?   f 12 sides?

2 What name do we give a triangle with:

   a three equal angles?
   b two equal sides?
   c all sides of different length?
   d two equal angles?

3 Draw a triangle with sides of 3 cm, 4 cm and 5 cm.
   What is special about one of its angles?
   What name do we give this type of triangle?

4 A shape has four edges.
   Both pairs of opposite edges are parallel.
   All of its edges are of equal length.
   Which of these names could we call it?

   a parallelogram   b rhombus
   c trapezium   d rectangle
   e kite   f square

5 Name each of these quadrilaterals.

   a   b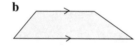

   c   d

6 Polygons can be either convex or concave.
   Which of these polygons are concave?

   a   b

   c   d

7 What does it mean if two shapes are said to be congruent.

8 Which of these shapes are congruent to Shape A.

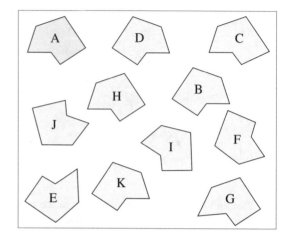

9 Explain how you can test for congruence.

10 Draw two shapes that are congruent but when you look at them they appear not to be congruent.

HOMEWORK S4

1 Copy this diagram.

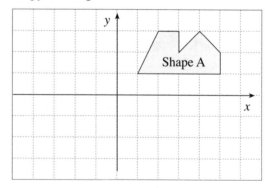

   a Reflect Shape A in the x-axis. Label it B.
   b Reflect Shape A in the y-axis. Label it C.

2 Draw a pair of axes with values of x and y from −5 to 5. Plot the points (2, 1), (2, 2), (3, 3), (4, 2), (5, 2), (5, 1). Join them in order.

   a Reflect the shape in the line $x = 2$.
   b Reflect the image in the line $y = -1$.

3 Copy this diagram.

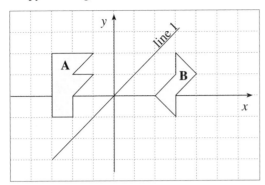

 a Reflect Shape A in line 1.
 b Reflect Shape B in line 1.

4 Plot the points (1, ⁻2,), (3, ⁻2), (2, ⁻3), (1, ⁻3).
Join them to make Shape C.

Reflect Shape C in the line $x = {}^-1$, reflect the image in the line $y = 1$.
List the coordinates of this final image.

HOMEWORK S5

1 Copy each shape and draw in all its lines of symmetry.

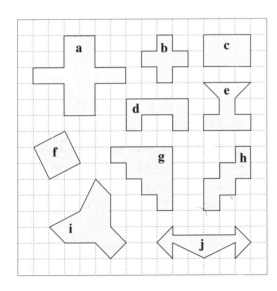

2 Draw an equilateral triangle.
On your triangle, draw in all its lines of symmetry.

3 On a square grid, draw a shape with nine squares that has:

 a no lines of symmetry
 b one line of symmetry
 c two lines of symmetry
 d four lines of symmetry.

4 Use all three of these pieces together to make symmetrical shapes.

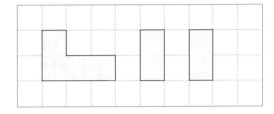

 a Draw three different shapes that each have one line of symmetry.
 b Draw a shape with two lines of symmetry.

5 A 4-letter word in capitals has letters with these lines of symmetry.

Letter 1	a horizontal and a vertical
Letter 2	a vertical
Letter 3	none
Letter 4	a horizontal

 a Find a word which fits all the clues.
 b Make up some symmetry clues for a word of your own.

HOMEWORK S6

1 a What is the order of rotational symmetry of this road sign?

 b How many lines of symmetry does the sign have?

2 Copy each of these signs, label its order of rotational symmetry, and draw in any lines of symmetry.

a b

c d

e f

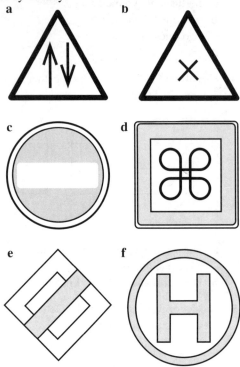

3 Draw a different sign with an order of rotational symmetry of:

  a two   **b** one.

4 The year 1881, when Alexander II was assassinated in Russia, has an order of rotational symmetry of 2.
Find some other years with an order of rotational symmetry of 2.

5 A 5-letter word in capitals has letters with these orders of rotational symmetry.

Letter 1	1
Letter 2	infinite
Letter 3	4
Letter 4	1
Letter 5	2

  a Find a word which fits all the clues.
  b Make up some rotational symmetry clues for a word of your own.

6 These tiles can be used as many times as you like to make larger shapes. Each shape must use at least two of the three different tiles.

Make a shape with an order of rotational symmetry of:

  a one   **b** two   **c** three   **d** four.

HOMEWORK S7

1 Measure each of these angles to the nearest degree.

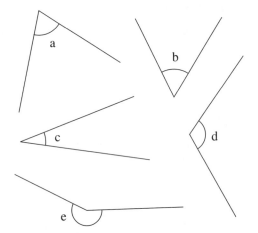

2 Draw accurately angles of these sizes.

  a 30°   **b** 67°   **c** 95°
  d 105°   **e** 17°   **f** 45°

3 In this diagram, state if each labelled angle is obtuse, reflex, acute or a right angle.

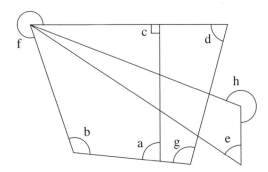

4 Draw accurately angles of these sizes.

   a 130°   **b** 175°   **c** 260°
   d 305°   **e** 284°   **f** 350°

5 **a** Draw a horizontal line.
   b Draw a line AB at an angle of 60° to the horizontal line.
   c Draw a line CD at right angles to line AB.
   d What is the angle between line CD and the horizontal line?

HOMEWORK S8

1 Calculate the angles marked with letters. In each case, line AB is straight.

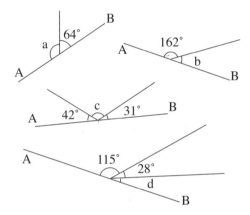

2 Calculate these missing angles.

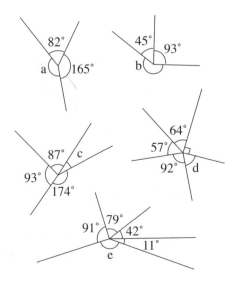

3 Each diagram shows two straight lines that cross. Give the angles marked with letters.

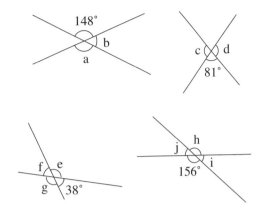

4 Each diagram below shows one pair of parallel lines. Give the angles marked with letters.

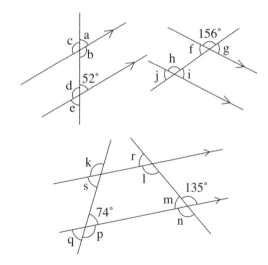

5 A book shelf was put up badly so that it made an angle of 3° to the horizontal.
At what angle was the shelf to the vertical?

HOMEWORK S9

1 Calculate the size of this missing angle.

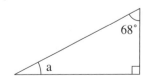

2 Calculate the labelled angles in each of these triangles.

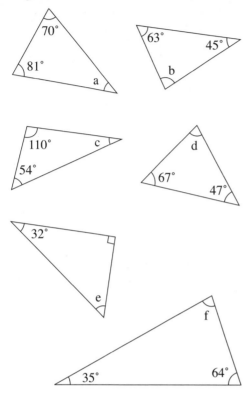

3 Calculate the missing angles in each diagram.

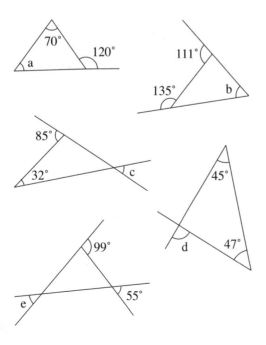

4 In these isosceles triangles, lines marked // are the same length.
Calculate the missing angles.

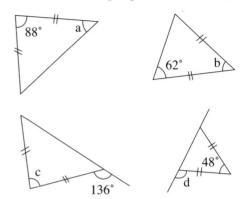

5 What is the size of an interior angle in an equilateral triangle?

6 A ladder has its base on a horizontal path. The ladder leans so that the top of it makes an angle of 32° to the vertical wall of a house.

  a Sketch the ground, ladder and wall, showing any known angles.
  b Calculate the angle that the ladder makes with the path.

HOMEWORK S10

1 Use only a ruler and a pair of compasses to construct triangles with these sides.

  a 5 cm, 8 cm, 6 cm
  b 4 cm, 9 cm, 7 cm
  c 57 mm, 48 mm, 64 mm
  d 9.5 cm, 5.9 cm, 4.7 cm
  e 5.4 cm, 3.3 cm, 7.5 cm

2 Construct each of these triangles. What is special about all of them?

  a 6.6 cm, 11.0 cm, 8.8 cm
  b 5 cm, 12 cm, 13 cm
  c 36 mm, 48 mm, 60 mm.

3 a Construct an equilateral triangle with sides of 8 cm.
  b What is the size of an interior angle in your triangle?

4 Sally was asked to construct a triangle with sides of 4 cm, 5 cm and 10 cm, but she refused. Why did she refuse?

5 a Using compasses and a protractor, construct a triangle ABC where AB = 6 cm, BC = 7 cm, and angle B = 50°.
  b What is the length of side AC?

6 a Using compasses and a protractor, construct a triangle PQR where angle Q = 45°, angle R = 60°, and QR = 5 cm.
  b What is the length of side PR?

HOMEWORK S11

1 Each square on the grid below is 1 cm by 1 cm.
  a What is the area of the shaded rectangle?

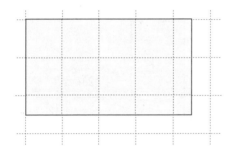

  b Calculate the perimeter of the rectangle.

2 A rectangular garden is 15 metres by 8 metres.
  a Calculate its area.
  b Calculate its perimeter.

3 Grass seed to sow one square metre costs 15p, and edging strip costs 86p a metre.
Leela wants to sow a piece of land 6 metres by 8.5 metres, and edge its perimeter.
  a Calculate the cost of grass seed.
  b Calculate the cost of edging strip.
  c Give the total cost.

4 Andy wants to varnish a wooden floor. The floor is 3.42 metres by 5.64 metres. A tin of varnish covers 9 square metres and costs £6.85

How much will the varnish cost Andy? Explain.

5 These are the dimensions of some rectangular sports pitches or courts.
Copy this table, and calculate the areas and perimeters.

Sport	Size (metres)	Area	Perimeter
Squash	9.75 by 6.40		
Hockey	91.4 by 54.9		
Basketball	28.6 by 14.0		
Soccer	90.1 by 45.9		
Badminton	13.4 by 6.1		

6 A rectangle has a perimeter of 20 cm and an area of 24 cm².
What are its length and width?

7 The width of a rectangular field is 174 metres and its area is 73 254 square metres.
How long is the field?

8 A rectangle has a perimeter of 23 cm and an area of 33 cm².
Calculate its length and width.

9 a A rectangle has a perimeter of 24 cm. Write down three different areas the rectangle could have.
  b What is the largest area possible for a rectangle with a perimeter of 24 cm?

HOMEWORK S12

1 Calculate the area of this triangle.

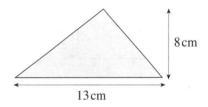

2 What is the area of this triangle?

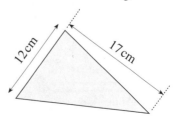

3 Calculate the area of this triangle.

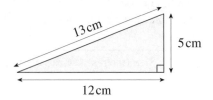

4 A triangle has an area of 96 cm² and a base length of 10 cm.
What is its height?

5 A farmer's field is shaped like a triangle.

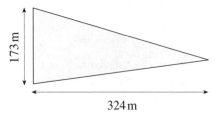

The farmer grows a crop of potatoes and expects a harvest of 11 kg from each square metre of land.
Calculate the weight of potatoes he expects to harvest from his field.

6 A garden is shaped like a right-angled triangle with its end cut off.
Calculate the area of the garden.

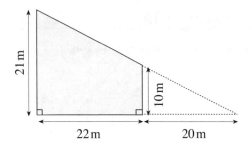

7 Calculate the area of this parallelogram.

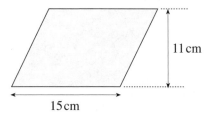

8 Calculate the area of this parallelogram.

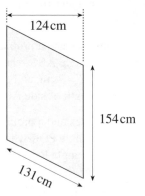

Homework S13

1 This is the plan of a room.
What are the dimensions a and b?

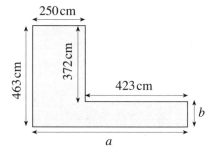

2 For this garden, calculate the missing dimensions a and b.

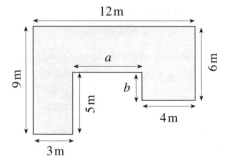

3 Calculate the area of this shape.

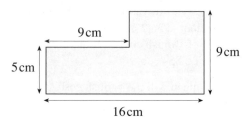

4   A piece of material is this shape.

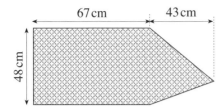

   a Calculate the area of the piece.
   b The material was cut from a larger rectangular piece 1½ metres long by ½ metre wide.
      What area of material was wasted?

5   A rectangular garden, 14 metres long by 6 metres wide, consists of a rectangular lawn with a path of width 150 cm all the way round it.

   a Calculate the area of the lawn.
   b Calculate the area of the path.

6   Amy is painting the wall below with two coats of emulsion paint.

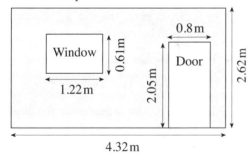

A 1 litre tin of emulsion covers 6 metres². How many tins would you advise Amy to buy? Explain.

7   Calculate the area of this garden.

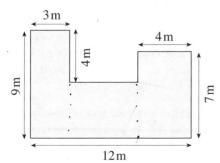

HOMEWORK S14

1 What mathematical name do we give the shape of a dice?

2 Give three examples of objects in the home shaped like a cylinder.

3 What mathematical name do we give each of these solids?

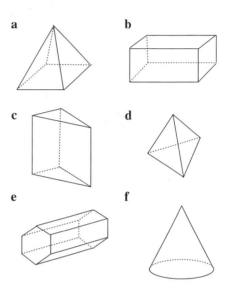

4 On dotty triangular paper, draw these solids.
   a a cube   b a cuboid

5 Name three solids that have curved surfaces.

6 A solid has two octagonal faces and eight rectangular faces.
   What mathematical name does it have?

7 Name two everyday objects which are shaped like each of these.
   a a sphere   b a cuboid
   c a triangular prism d a cone

8 How many faces, edges and vertices has a cuboid?

9 A solid has four faces, four vertices and six edges. What solid could this be?

10 Draw: a a triangular-based prism
          b a triangular-based pyramid.

HOMEWORK S15

1. On centimetre squared paper, draw a full-size net of:
   a. a cube with sides of 3 cm
   b. a cuboid with sides of 2 cm, 3 cm and 4 cm.

2. a. What solid has this net?

   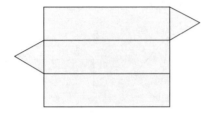

   b. Sketch a different net for the same solid.

3. Pentominoes are shapes made from five joined squares. P and Q are two examples.

   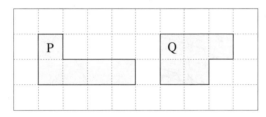

   a. Only one of these examples is the net of an open-topped cube. Which one?
   b. On squared paper, draw six other different pentominoes. Label any that are nets of an open-topped cube.

4. The dots on an ordinary dice are positioned so that the numbers of dots on opposite faces add up to 7.
   Draw a net of a 2 cm dice, showing all the dots in their correct positions.

5. Mary claims she can colour the net of any solid using just two colours so that no two faces that touch are the same colour.
   a. Try this with some nets of your own.
   b. Do you think Mary is right, or would she sometimes need a third colour?

HOMEWORK S16

1. Calculate the surface area of this cuboid.

   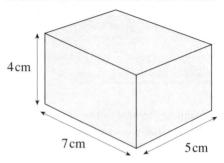

2. What is the surface area of a cube that has an edge length of 7 cm?

3. Find the surface area of cuboids with these dimensions?
   a. 5 metres by 8 metres by 3 metres
   b. 2 cm by 3.5 cm by 16 cm
   c. 200 cm by 4000 cm by 80 metres

4. A cube has a surface area of 216 cm². Calculate the length of each edge?

5. A large dice is in the shape of a 25 cm cube. The cube is to be sprayed with paint.
   a. Find the surface area of the cube.

   With 6 ml of paint you can cover 5 cm².

   b. How much paint is needed for the dice?

6. A cuboid is made from a sheet of card that is 20 cm long and 18 cm wide.

   The cuboid is 5 cm wide, 3 cm high and 9 cm long and is made with no glue flaps.
   a. Sketch the cuboid.
   b. Calculate the surface area of the cuboid.
   c. Sketch a net for the cuboid.
   d. On a sketch show how your net can be cut from a 20 cm x 18 cm sheet of card.
   e. Calculate the area of card wasted from the sheet when the cuboid is made.

7. A cuboid has a surface area of 264 cm². The cuboid is 6 cm high and 6 cm wide. Find the length of the cuboid.

8 Jake made a cuboid which was 6 cm wide, 6 cm high and 9 cm long.

Sketch and label a cuboid that has roughly the same surface area as Jake's.

HOMEWORK S17

1 Draw a net for a cuboid with dimensions 3cm, 4cm, and 5cm.
You do not need glue flaps on your net.

2 a Sketch a net for a model of this shape.

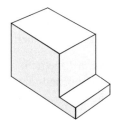

  b Make a model of the shape.

3 Visualise this solid.

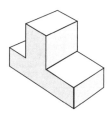

Sketch its front, side, and plan views.

4 These are three views of a solid.

Front view   Side view

Plan

Sketch the solid.

5 Sketch a plan, a side view, and a front view for this solid.

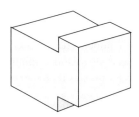

6 a Make four different shapes by joining five multi-link cubes.
  b Sketch each shape you make.
  c For each shape draw a plan, a side, and a front view.

7 Visualise a triangular prism.

  a Draw a plan, a side view, and a front view of your prism.
  b How many vertices, faces and edges has your prism.
  c Make your prism.

HOMEWORK S18

1 Convert:

  a 3.6 metres to centimetres
  b 1567 centimetres to metres
  c 675 millimetres to centimetres
  d 4 metres to millimetres
  e 54 centimetres to millimetres
  f 4.2 kilometres to metres
  g 12 million centimetres to kilometres
  h 1.2 kilometres to millimetres.

2 Copy and complete this table.

mm	cm	m	km
1200			0.0012
	34		
		17.4	
			0.34

3 The weight of a £1 coin is 9.5 grams. Give this as a weight in kilograms.

4 Convert:

   a 167 minutes to hours and minutes
   b 6 $\frac{1}{4}$ hours to minutes
   c 5 $\frac{1}{2}$ minutes to seconds
   d 1 hour 7 minutes to seconds
   e 8000 seconds to hours, minutes and seconds
   f 740 hours to days and hours.

5 A floor tile is 152 mm wide.

   a How many tiles will fit across the width of a room that is 6.5 metres wide?
   b What space is left over for joints between the tiles?

6 A young man claimed he had been alive for a billion (thousand million) seconds. How old would this make him?

Homework S19

The chart below gives some conversions for changing from Imperial to metric units
Use it for all the questions in this homework

    1 inch = 2.54 cm
    1 yard = 0.914 m
    1 mile = 1.61 km
    1 pint = 0.568 litre
    1 gallon = 4.546 litres
    1 pound (lb) = 0.4536 kg
    1 ton = 1.016 tonnes

1 Anita is 5 feet 4 inches tall.
There are 12 inches in a foot.
Roughly what is her height in centimetres?

2 From the information above, roughly how many pints are in a gallon?

3 **a** What is 84 miles per hour in km per hour?
    b What is 312 km per hour in miles per hour?

4 A cricket pitch is 22 yards long.
One kilometre is equivalent to the length of roughly how many cricket pitches?

5 A table is 840 mm wide.
Convert this distance to inches.

6 The capacity of a fuel tank is 1200 litres.
Heating fuel costs 80p per gallon.
What is the cost of filling the tank with fuel?

7 A rectangle measures 5 inches by 4 inches.

   a What is its area in square inches?
   b Calculate its area in square centimetres.
   c How many square centimetres are equivalent to one square inch?

8 The diameter of Jupiter is 143 800 kilometres.
The diameter of the Earth is 7928 miles.
How many times greater is Jupiter's diameter than the diameter of Earth?

9 A metal pipe weighs 7.26 lb per yard.
What is its weight in kg per metre?

10 There are 1000 kg in 1 metric tonne.
Calculate how many pounds are in 1 Imperial ton.

Homework S20

1 Copy this diagram.

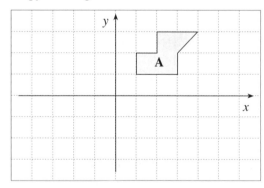

   a Rotate Shape A 90° anticlockwise with (0, 0) as the centre of rotation.
   b Rotate Shape A 90° clockwise about (1, 1).

2 Draw a pair of axes with values of x from $^-5$ to 5 and values of y from $^-8$ to 8.
Plot the points (2, 1), (2, 3), (3, 3), (4, 2), (5, 2), (5, 1), (3, 0) and join them in order.
Label the shape A.

Rotate Shape A:
   a 90° anticlockwise about the point (0, 1).
   b 180° using (1, 0) as the centre of rotation.

3 Copy this diagram

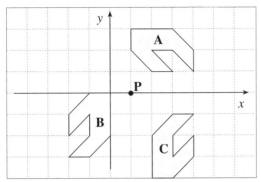

   a Give the rotation that maps A onto B.
   b What rotation maps A onto C?
   c What rotation maps B onto A?
   d Shape D is a rotation of A by 270°
      clockwise about P. Draw and label shape D.

4 Give a rotation that has the same effect as a
   rotation of 90° clockwise about (-3, 2).

5 On a pair of axes plot the points (0, 2), (0, 1),
   (1, 0), (1, -1), (2, -1), (3, 0), (2, 1), (1, 1).
   Join the points in order, label the shape A.

   a Give the coordinates of the image of A after
      a 90° rotation anticlockwise about (-2, -2).
   b Find the area of Shape A.
   c Explain what happens to the area of a shape
      when it is rotated.

Homework S21

1 a Estimate what fraction of the petrol tank is
      filled with fuel.

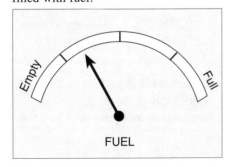

   b The tank holds 48 litres when full.
      Estimate the number of litres that
      can be added.

2 A barometer dial is marked round the outside
   with these weather zones:
   Stormy, *Rain*, *Change*, *Fair* and *Very Dry*.

   Each zone depends on the air pressure.

   Stormy   between 950 mb and 970 mb
   Rain   between 970 mb and 985 mb
   Change   between 985 mb and 1008 mb
   Fair   between 1008 mb and 1032 mb
   Very Dry between 1032 mb and 1050 mb

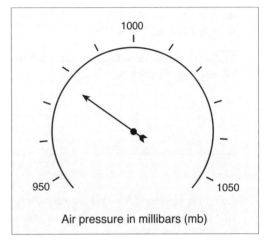

Air pressure in millibars (mb)

   a Which zone is the hand pointing to?
   b Make a copy of the dial, and colour and
      label the different weather zones.

3 What reading do each of the pointers show on
   these scales?

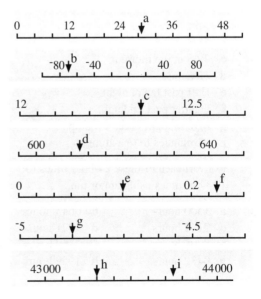

4 What value does the pointer show on this scale when:

a A = 10 and B = 15?
b A = 42 and B = 44?
c A = 10.65 and B = 10.7?
d A = ⁻30 and B = 20?
e A = 1480 and B = 1500?

5 Make six copies (**a** to **f**) of the scale below, but do **not** write in the letters A and B.

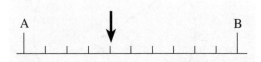

Label the positions A and B with numbers so that the pointer reads:
a 175   b 8.5   c ⁻5
d 0.0075   e 2375   f ⁻125.
Different answers are possible

HOMEWORK S22

1 Convert each of these times to 24-hour times.

a 3 pm
b 5 am
c 7:45 in the morning
d 12 noon
e Half past ten at night
f Quarter past midnight
g Five to eight in the evening
h 17 minutes to one at night

2 Convert each of these 24-hour times to 12-hour times using am or pm.

a 1500 hours   b 0645 hours
c 2145 hours   d 1721 hours
e 0005 hours   f 2359 hours
g 0432 hours   h 1959 hours

3 What time is 2 hours and 17 minutes later than each of these times?
Write each answer in the same style as the question is written

a 4:30 am
b 1815 hours
c Five to seven at night
d 11:20 am
e 2321 hours
f Quarter to midnight

4 The reflection of a 12-hour clock, with hands but without numbers, appears to show the time of 7:53.
What is the true time?

5 The two hands of a 12-hour clock are in line once every hour.
For example, at 12 o'clock and just after 3:16 the two hands are in line.
Give two times after 7 o'clock when the hands are also in line.

6 Sian started her journey at 11:23 am and completed it at 2:15 pm.
How long did Sian's journey take?

7 Mike works exactly 38 hours each week, and takes one hour off for lunch every day.
The timesheet below shows his start and finish times for week 24.

Timesheet for week 24	
Monday	8:45 am till 4:50 pm
Tuesday	8:20 am till 5:10 pm
Wednesday	9:15 am till 4:23 pm
Thursday	8:45 am till 6:07 pm

He starts work at 7:45 am on Friday, his last working day of the week.
At what time on Friday does he finish?

HOMEWORK S23

The timetable below shows the first five trains on weekdays from Salington to Crewby
Use it for all the questions in this homework

Salington to Crewby				Weekdays	
	A	B	C	D	E
Salington	0643	0714	0744	0813	0845
Tanbury	0654	0726	0753	0824	0854
Wedley	0657	0731	0759	0827	0859
Motting	0704	0740	0801	0834	0905
Welgrove	0710	0748	0809	0840	0912
Panwell	0724	0804	0827	0854	0925
Crewby	0740	0822	0843	0910	0941

1. What time does train A arrive at Tanbury?

2. When does train E arrive at Panwell?

3. How many trains arrive at Tanbury before 8 am?

4. Which train arrives at Motting at about half past eight?

5. When does the 8:27 train from Wedley arrive at Welgrove?

6. How long does train B take to travel from:
    a Salington to Motting?
    b Tanbury to Welgrove?
    c Motting to Panwell?
    d Wedley to Crewby?

7. How long does train D take to travel from Salington to Crewby?

8. Which train travels between Salington and Crewby in the shortest time?

9. Siobhan arrives at Motting station at a quarter to eight to travel to Panwell.
    a How long must she wait for the next train?
    b What time will she arrive in Panwell?

10. a List the journey times between Welgrove and Panwell for the first five trains.
    b By how many minutes do the times vary?
    c Which is the slowest train, and by how many minutes?

HOMEWORK S24

1. Copy this diagram.

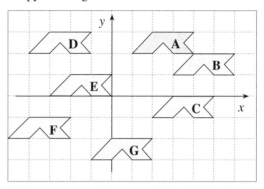

Each shape is a translation of Shape A.
Give the translation that maps Shape A on to each of the shapes B to G.

2. Using the diagram for question **1**, copy and complete this table.

Translation	Vector
E to B	■
C to D	■
F to B	■
G to D	■
C to F	■
E to G	■
G to A	■

3. Explain what the inverse of a vector is.
Give an example and draw a diagram.

4. On a pair of axes plot the points (3, 1), (1, 1), (2, 2), (2, 3), (3, 2).
Join the points in order and label the shape A.

Translate Shape A by each of these vectors:

a $\begin{pmatrix} -2 \\ -1 \end{pmatrix}$ label the image B.

b $\begin{pmatrix} 0 \\ -5 \end{pmatrix}$ label the image C.

c $\begin{pmatrix} -5 \\ 2 \end{pmatrix}$ label the image D.

5. Write a short report to explain *translations* to someone who has never heard of the term.

Handling Data

Homework D1

1

7W Survey - Favourite Pets

Pet	Tally	Total
Budgie	II	2
Cat	IIII II	7
Dog	III	3
Hamster	IIII	5
Rabbit	IIII IIII I	11
Grand Total		28

a How many pupils in class 7W chose cat?
b Which pet did five pupils choose?
c Which pet is the most popular with pupils in 7W?

2

7Y Favourite Pets

Dog   Hamster   Cat   Cat   Dog
Cat   Cat   Hamster   Guinea Pig
Cat   Dog   Dog   Cat   Cat   Cat
Hamster   Cat   Hamster   Dog
Guinea Pig   Hamster   Cat   Dog
Dog   Hamster   Cat   Guinea Pig

a Copy and complete the tally chart below to show this data for class 7Y.

7Y Survey - Favourite Pets

Pet	Tally	Total
Cat		
Dog		
Guinea Pig		
Hamster		
Grand Total		27

b How many pupils in 7Y chose dog?
c Which pet is the most popular?
d Dawn says the chart shows that the guinea pig is the least popular pet with 7Y pupils. Explain why Dawn is wrong.

3

7X Favourite Pets

Cat   Tortoise   Cat   Budgie   Dog
Cat   Dog   Hamster   Guinea Pig
Tortoise   Cat   Rabbit   Dog   Rabbit
Rabbit   Dog   Cat   Cat   Hamster
Guinea Pig   Cat   Dog   Guinea Pig
Dog   Hamster   Dog   Dog   Rabbit

a Make a tally chart to show this data.
b How many pupils are there in class 7X?
c How many different types of pet did the pupils choose?
d How many pupils chose tortoise?
e How many chose hamster or guinea pig?

4 Use the data from questions **1**, **2** and **3** to show all three Year 7 classes in one table.

5

Cyclists' Survey - Ages

23 28 44 50 47 18 69 33 33 37
67 65 35 38 48 43 51 46 30 14
44 49 10 66 61 58 30 24 28 44
29 56 35 38 35 23 65 21 37 11
27 34 14 44 49 47 36 33 28 52

a Copy and complete this frequency table.

Cyclists' Survey

Age	Tally	Total
10 - 19		
20 - 29		
30 - 39		
40 - 49		
50 - 59		
60 - 69		
Grand Total		

b How many cyclists took part in the survey?
c How many are in the 60 - 69 age group?
d How many teenagers are in the survey?
e Which age group has the most cyclists?

HOMEWORK D2

1

Distances travelled by delivery vans in 5 days	
Kilometres	frequency
100 – 199	3
200 – 299	5
300 – 399	8
400 – 499	12
500 – 599	21
600 – 699	18
700 – 799	4

a How many vans travelled between 200 km and 299 km in the five days?
b Which distance has the highest frequency?
c Which class has a frequency of 4?

How many vans travelled:
d less than 500 km?
e at least 300 km?
f less than 250 km?
g Explain your answer to part **f**.

2 People were asked to estimate one minute. Tests were timed in seconds and this data was collected.

Estimates of one minute (seconds)

46, 51, 38, 44, 57, 65, 71, 54, 49, 68, 53, 47
74, 58, 55, 62, 41, 59, 60, 63, 56, 52, 58, 66
49, 54, 63, 68, 72, 56, 64, 60, 55, 48, 51, 62
59, 66, 52, 58, 61, 67, 54, 56, 59, 62, 46, 50

a How many people took part in the test?
b Make a grouped frequency table for the data.
  Use groups of, 35 – 39, 40 – 44, 45 – 49, 50 – 54, 55 – 59, 60 – 64, 65 – 69, 70 – 74
c Which group has the highest frequency?
d Which groups have a frequency of 6?
e Make a second grouped frequency table for the data.
  Use groups; 36 – 45, 46 – 55, 56 – 65 etc.
f Which group has the highest frequency now?

3 In a library survey people were asked to give their age in years.
This is the data that was collected.

Age (years) of library users.

14, 22, 35, 44, 34, 19, 15, 21, 18, 17, 65, 70,
29, 33, 62, 56, 45, 49, 58, 62, 76, 55, 63, 38,
42, 31, 19, 18, 18, 29, 16, 62, 47, 17, 28, 51,
64, 27, 31, 40, 61, 19, 20, 26, 43, 18, 20, 22,
15, 12, 19, 24, 11, 15, 18, 23, 34, 35, 18, 10

a How many people gave data on their age?
b Give the age of the oldest user.
c Make a grouped frequency table for the data.
  Use groups of: 10 – 19, 20 – 29, 30 – 39, 40 – 49, 50 – 59, 60 – 69, 70 – 79.

From your table:
d Which group had the highest frequency?
e How many users were at least 40 years old?
f How many uses were younger than 30?
g Explain why your table will not help you answer the question:
  '*How many users were 65 or older?*'
h Make a different grouped frequency table where one of the age groups is 65 – 74.
i Now answer the question in **part g**.

4 In a grouped frequency table it is important that the groups or classes are of equal size.

A set of data D has a lowest value of 28 and a highest value of 67.
a Give three different ways you could group the data.

You have to answer a question about how many pieces of data in D were greater than 45.
b What groups might you choose for this?

This is a line from a grouped frequency table for the data set D.

Group	Frequency
36 – 40	19

c Explain what this line of the table does tell you and what it cannot tell you?

HOMEWORK D3

1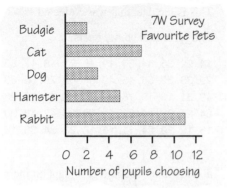

  a How many pupils in 7W chose rabbit?
  b Which pet did two pupils choose?
  c How many pupils chose cat or dog?

2 Use the data from Homework **D2** question **2** to draw a bar chart for the 7Y survey.

3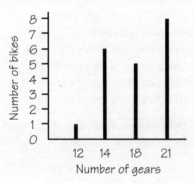

  a How many bikes in the survey have 14 gears?
  b Which number of gears is the most popular?
  c How many bikes are in the survey?

4

Road Bike Survey - Number of gears

18 14 18 12 14 14 7 18 18 12
7 14 18 14 14 12 6 18 6 7
14 7 12 14 12 18 12 7 18 14

  a Make a tally chart for this data.
  b Draw a bar-line graph to show this data.
  c Which number of gears is the most popular for road bikes in the survey?

5

Mountain Bike Survey

Make	Total
Claud Butler	3
Falcon	5
Muddy Fox	6
Raleigh	4
Others	2

Draw a bar chart for this mountain bike survey.

6

Mountain Bike Survey
Size of frame (cm)

53 46 38 46 53
51 46 51 48 51
53 51 51 48 53
56 53 38 51 51

  a Make a tally chart for this data.
  b Draw a bar-line graph to show this data.

HOMEWORK D4

1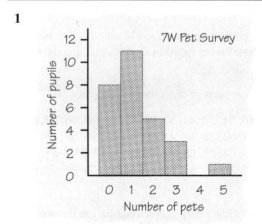

  a How many pupils in class 7W have 1 pet?
  b How many pupils have at least 2 pets?

2

A class has 27 pupils.
The most popular number of pets is 1.
No pupil has more than 4 pets.
14 pupils have at least 2 pets.
Twice as many pupils have 1 pet as 3 pets.

Draw a possible bar chart for this class.

3

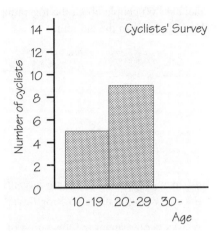

Copy and complete this bar chart, using the data from Homework **D2** question **5**.

4 The line graph below shows the results of pet surveys for classes 7W and 7X.

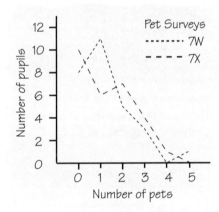

a How many pupils in 7X have no pets?
b How many pupils are there in 7X?
c Which class has more pupils with 3 pets?

5

No. of pets	No. of pupils	
	7Y	7Z
0	7	5
1	5	9
2	8	7
3	4	3
4	2	1
5	1	0
6	0	2

Draw a line graph to show these results.

HOMEWORK D5

1

Year 7 Merit Badges
Autumn Term

7W △ △ △ △ △

7X △ △ △

7Y △ △ △ ◁

7Z △ △ △ △ ◁

△ represents 2 badges

a How many merit badges did class 7X receive in the autumn term?
b How many merit badges did 7Z receive?
c How many badges were awarded in total?

2

Number of merit badges				
	7W	7X	7Y	7Z
Spring term	8	10	8	7
Summer term	9	8	7	9

Draw a pictogram, similar to the one in question **1**, to show the badges awarded in:
a the spring term
b the summer term.

3

Year 7 Absences
Summer Term

7W ◯ ◯ ◯ ◯ ◯ ◖

7X ◯ ◯ ◯ ◯ ◯ ◯

7Y ◯ ◯ ◯ ◯ ◖

7Z ◯ ◯ ◯ ◯ ◯ ◔

◯ represents 4 absences

a How many absences did class 7W have in the summer term?
b How many absences did 7Z have?
c How many absences were there altogether?
d Write down how you could show that a class had 21 absences.

4

Number of absences				
	7W	7X	7Y	7Z
Autumn term	24	22	27	25
Spring term	40	36	44	46

   a Draw a pictogram, similar to the one in question **3**, to show the number of absences for the autumn term.

   b Draw a pictogram to show the number of absences for the spring term, using this key.

 represents 8 absences

5 Jessica is drawing a pictogram to show the number of coins pupils have on them. She decides to use this key.

 represents 5 coins

Explain why this key might be difficult to use.

HOMEWORK D6

1 Clare is doing a survey on duvets.
She asks 80 people about the tog-rating of the duvet they use in the summer.

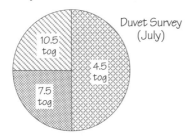

   a What is the most popular duvet in July?
   b How many people use a 4.5 tog duvet?
   c Copy and complete this table.

Duvet Survey - July

Duvet	4.5 tog	7.5 tog	10.5 tog
Number of people			

2 Michael asks 60 people about the tog-rating of the duvet they use in the autumn.

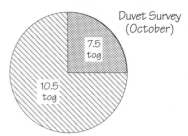

   a How many people use a 7.5 tog duvet?
   b How many people use a 10.5 tog duvet?

3 Tracey asks people about the tog-rating of the duvet they use in the winter.

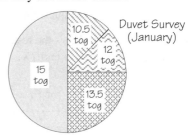

10 people use a 13.5 tog duvet.
   a How many people did Tracey ask?
   b How many people use a 12 tog duvet?
   c Copy and complete this table.

Duvet Survey - January

Duvet	10.5 tog	12 tog	13.5 tog	15 tog
Number of people				

4 a Draw a sketch to show each of the pie charts in questions **1**, **2** and **3**.

Graham asks people about the tog-rating of the duvet they use in April.

   b Sketch a pie chart to show what the results of Graham's survey might look like.

5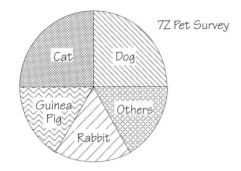

Pupils in class 7X have 36 pets altogether.
a How many dogs do pupils in 7X have?
b How many rabbits do pupils have?
c Copy and complete this table.

Pet	Total
Cat	
Dog	
Guinea Pig	
Rabbit	
Others	

6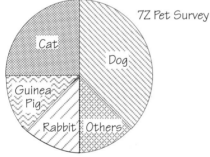

Pupils in class 7Z have 12 cats.
a How many pets do the pupils have in total?
b How many guinea pigs do the pupils have?
c Copy and complete this table.

Pet	Total
Cat	
Dog	
Guinea Pig	
Rabbit	
Others	

HOMEWORK D7

1 Jack draws a bar chart to show the favourite pets of the pupils in class 7A.

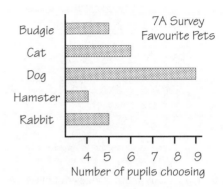

a How many pupils chose hamster?
b How many pupils chose rabbit?
c Carla looks at Jack's chart and says that rabbits were twice as popular as hamsters. Why do you think Carla said that?
d Draw a better bar chart to show this data.

2 Sian draws a bar-line graph to show the results of a mountain bike survey.

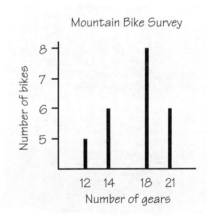

a How many bikes in the survey have 12 gears?
b How many bikes in the survey have more than 14 gears?
c Give two reasons why this bar-line graph has been badly drawn.
d Draw a better bar-line graph to show this data.

3 Emma draws a pictogram to show the number of merit badges awarded in the autumn term.

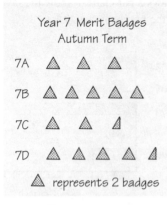

represents 2 badges

a How many merit badges did class 7A receive in the autumn term?
b How many merit badges did 7D receive?
c Carl looks at Emma's pictogram and says that 7D received the most merit badges. Why do you think Carl said that?
d Draw a better pictogram to show this data.

4 Martin draws a pictogram to show the number of absences in the summer term for Year 7.

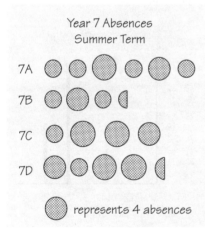

represents 4 absences

a How many absences did class 7B have in the summer term?
b How many absences did 7D have?
c How many absences were there altogether?
d Describe the mistake Martin has made in drawing this pictogram.
e Draw a better pictogram to show this data.

HOMEWORK D8

1
```
       7A Survey
Number of pets owned by each pupil

 0  2  1  0  4  2  2  3  2  0
 2  0  3  1  2  1  5  1  3  2
 1  1  2  0  0  2  3  4
```

a How many pupils are in class 7A?
b How many pets do they own altogether?
c Calculate the mean number of pets.

2
```
       7B Survey
Number of pets owned by each pupil

  1  3  2  2  0  4  5  0  1
   1  0  4  1  3  1  4  3
  3  1  0  3  1  2  2  0
```

a How many pupils are in 7B?
b How many pets do the pupils in 7B own?
c Calculate the mean number of pets.

3 a Which of the two classes has the higher total number of pets?
   b Explain why 7B has a higher mean number of pets than 7A.

4 a Make a tally chart to show the data in question 1.
   b Which number of pets is the mode for 7A?
   c Make a tally chart to show the data in question 2.
   d Which is the modal number of pets for 7B?

5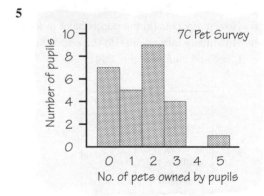

Which number of pets is the mode for 7C?

6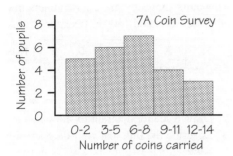

Which number of coins is the modal group?

7

	Number of pupils	Number of coins	Value of the coins
7A	28	168	£40.60
7B	25	160	£40.25
7C	26	169	£35.36
7D	24	162	£34.56

a Calculate the mean number of coins per pupil for each of the four classes.
b In which class, on average, do pupils carry the most coins?
c Calculate the mean value of coins per pupil for each class.
d In which class, on average, do pupils carry the most money with them?
e For 7A: £40.60 ÷ 168 = £0.24 (to 2 dp). Explain what this mean value is.

HOMEWORK D9

1 Sophie divides her 12 friends into 2 groups: 7 girls and 5 boys.
She asks them how much money they receive each week from pocket money, odd jobs, etc. The amounts for the girls are:

Girls £4.50 £3.40 £4.10 £3.50
£3.60 £9.60 £4.20

a List the data in order.
b Calculate the range of the amounts.
c Find the median amount.
d Calculate the mean amount.
e Explain why the median is a better average to use for this data than the mean.

2 The weekly amounts for the boys are:

Boys £4.30 £3.20 £5.40
£2.80 £3.90

a List the amounts in order.
b Calculate the range of the amounts.
c Find the median amount.

3 Use the values for the median and the range from questions **1** and **2** to compare Sophie's two groups of friends.

4

	SuperBowl Tenpin Bowling Points scoresheet			
Frame	Zoe	Tim	Steve	Deb
1	8	3	9	11
2	9	2	15	8
3	7	7	8	0
4	13	0	18	8
5	8	1	9	16
6	14	0	8	7
7	9	6	24	7
8	7	8	9	12
9	9	9	16	9
10	12	5	9	17

a For each bowler, calculate the range of the points scored.
b Whose scores are most closely grouped?
c Whose scores are most widely spread?

5 a List Zoe's scores in order, smallest first.
b Find Zoe's median number of points.
c Find the median number of points for each of the other three bowlers.
d Who scored the most points on average?

6 Use the values for the median and the range from questions **4** and **5** to compare the points scored by the four bowlers.

7 In 4 frames, James scores a total of 40 points. The range of his scores is 11 points, and his median number of points is 9.5
List his possible frame scores.

8 Make up a similar puzzle of your own for:
a 5 frames   b 6 frames.

HOMEWORK D10

1. *Aqua Swimming Club* has 7 junior members: Anna, Ben, Chris, Dipak, Eve, Fiona, Gary.
   Of these swimmers, Anna (A) is:
   2nd fastest at 50 metres freestyle,
   3rd fastest at 100 metres freestyle.

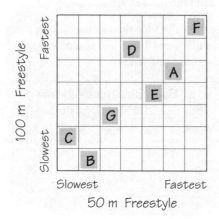

   a Copy and complete this sentence:
       Eve (E) is ____ fastest at 50 m freestyle,
       and ____ fastest at 100 m freestyle.
   b Who is fastest at both events?
   c Who is faster at 50 m, Ben or Chris?
   d Who is faster at 100 m, Ben or Chris?
   e Describe the link that the diagram shows between the swimmers' speeds in the 50 m and their speeds in the 100 m.
   f Which swimmers, when compared to the others, are equally good at the 100 m and the 50 m?
   g Dipak claims he is the only swimmer who is better at the 100 m than the 50 m. Explain why Dipak is wrong to say this.

2. This table shows the fastest swimmers in the 50 m freestyle and 200 m freestyle events.

	A	B	C	D	E	F	G
50 m	2nd	6th	7th	4th	3rd	1st	5th
200 m	5th	7th	3rd	1st	6th	2nd	4th

   a Draw a scatter diagram to show this data.
   b Is the link between the swimmers' speeds in the events as strong as the link between the events in question **1**?

3. This table shows the fastest swimmers in the 50 m freestyle and 1500 m freestyle events.

	A	B	C	D	E	F	G
50 m	2nd	6th	7th	4th	3rd	1st	5th
1500 m	7th	3rd	1st	4th	5th	6th	2nd

   a Draw a scatter diagram to show this data.
   b Describe the link that your diagram shows between the swimmers' speeds in the 50 m and their speeds in the 1500 m.

4. This table shows the fastest swimmers at 100 m and the fastest runners at 100 m.

	A	B	C	D	E	F	G
Swim	3nd	7th	6th	2nd	4th	1st	5th
Run	2nd	5th	1st	6th	7th	3rd	4th

   a Draw a scatter diagram to show this data.
   b Does your diagram show any link between speeds of swimming and running?

HOMEWORK D11

1. Dean buys a £1 ticket for the National Lottery.

   Use this scale to match P, Q, R, S and T with the likelihood that:

   a the last individual jackpot winner was female
   b the numbers drawn will all be under 50
   c Dean will win £10
   d at least one of the numbers drawn will be in the 40s
   e the jackpot will not be won this week.

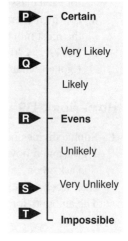

2. a Make up three statements of your own about the National Lottery.
   b Draw a scale like the one in question **1**.
   c Use your scale to show the likelihood of each of your statements.

3

```
0%        50%        100%
|----------|----------|
```

a Copy this scale.

b Estimate the chance that each of the following things will happen and show them on your scale.

  A It will rain tomorrow
  B Tomorrow will be sunny
  C It will snow tomorrow

4 Luke's aunt is expecting a baby.

a Luke says there is a 50% chance she will have a girl.
Do you agree with Luke? Explain.

b Luke also says there is a 50% chance the baby will be right-handed.
Do you agree with Luke? Explain.

5 Damon is going away for the weekend.
The weather forecast says there is:
  a 40% chance of rain on Saturday, and
  a 60% chance of rain on Sunday.
Damon is disappointed because he thinks this means he is 100% certain to get some rain.
Do you agree with Damon? Explain.

HOMEWORK D12

1 If you flip a coin, you have a 50% chance of getting a head.
What is the chance of getting a tail?

2 Reza flips a coin twice and gets two heads.
If she flips the coin again, what is the chance she will get another head?

3 The numbers on an ordinary dice are:

  1 2 3 4 5 6

In one throw of the dice, there is a 50% chance of scoring more than 3.
Which of these also have a 50% chance of being scored in one throw?

a an even number
b a number less than 3
c an odd number
d a prime number

4 A game uses a special roller dice.
The numbers on the dice are:

  0 1 2 3 4 6

In one roll, the chance of scoring 0 is:
  1 out of 6

Give the chance of scoring:
a 2   **b** more than 3
c 3 or more   **d** less than 6
e an even number **f** an odd number.

5 The numbers on this roller dice are:

  1 2 3 4 5 6 8 10

In one roll, the probability of scoring 10 is:
  $1/8$

Give the probability of scoring:
a more than 6   **b** less than 6
c 6 or more   **d** an odd number
e an even number **f** a prime number.

6 Ruth holds a raffle in aid of Comic Relief.
The details of the raffle are:

  Number of prizes donated   5
  Number of tickets sold   50
  No ticket can win more than 1 prize

James buys one ticket.

a What is the probability he will win a prize?
b What is the probability James will win the first prize?
c If James does not win first prize, what is the probability he will win second prize?
d If James does not win any of the first four prizes, what is the probability he will win the last prize?

7 Mark holds a similar raffle with 5 prizes and 50 tickets, but each ticket in his raffle can win any number of prizes.
Sarah buys one ticket.

a What is the probability Sarah will win the first prize?
b What is the probability Sarah will win the last prize?

Revision and Solving Problems

Homework R1

Do not use a calculator for this homework

1. What number is 21 less than five million?

2. Subtract three hundred and fifty thousand from three and a quarter million.

3. a Add: 345, 6, 19, 1085, and 9
   b Find the sum of 23 677 and 5876
   c Find the difference between 10 095 and 3588
   d What is the product of 24 and 374?
   e 576 944 ÷ 8
   f 15 574 + 208 − 13 788

4. A crate of orange juice holds 18 cartons. A supermarket buys 3500 crates. How many cartons is this?

5. A case of cat food holds 24 tins.
   a How many cases can be filled from 17 500 tins?
   b How many tins will be left over?

6. Find the sum of the first seven prime numbers.

7. List the prime numbers between 80 and 100.

8. List the first five multiples of 9.

9. Is 15 777 a multiple of 9? Explain how you can tell.

10. List all the factors of 36.

11. Which factors of 120 are also factors of 48?

12. List the prime factors of 160.

13. Round these numbers to the nearest 10.

    a 58   b 275   c 72
    d 108   e 10 506   f 7

14. List all the whole numbers that, when rounded to the nearest 10, give an answer of 300.

15. Rounded to the nearest 1000, the attendance at a football match was 32 000.

    What is the largest the attendance might be?

Homework R2

Do not use a calculator for this homework

1. By rounding, estimate each of the answers ■.

   a 147 + 282 = ■   b 675 − 428 = ■
   c 37 × 58 = ■   d 236 ÷ 77 = ■

2. Joel runs 17 miles every day of the week. Estimate the total number of miles he runs in six weeks.

3. A minibus seats 18 passengers. Estimate how many minibuses are needed to take 656 fans to a rugby match.

4. A garden centre sells seeds in packets of 24. Estimate the number of seeds needed to fill 285 packets.

5. Copy the calculation: $9 + 5 \times 3 \div 6 =$
   Put in brackets to give an answer of 4.

6. Copy and complete using BODMAS rules:

   a $5 \times 8 - 3 =$ b $56 \div 7 + 1 =$
   c $12 - 4 + 9 \div 3 =$ d $15 \times 8 - 6 =$
   e $9 \times (12 - 9) =$ f $(29 - 5) \div (11 - 3) =$

7. In this calculation, replace each ■ with a number.

   $$(■ + ■) \times (■ - ■) = 55$$

8. Find the value of:

   a $55 - 7^2$ b $24 + 3^2$
   c $8^2 - 58$ d $9^2 - 7^2$

9. Which is larger, one million or 10^5? Explain.

10. Copy and complete each of these.

    a $(20 - 3^2) \times 4 =$ b $48 \div (24 - 4^2) =$
    c $(5^2 - 3^2) \div 4 =$ d $(6^2 - 2^2) \div 3^2 =$

11. Which gives the larger answer: doubling a number then adding 4, or adding 4 then doubling? Explain.

HOMEWORK R3

Do not use a calculator for this homework

1. List these numbers in order.
   Start with the smallest

   5.15   5.06   5.252   5.3   5.00055

2. In the number 27.654, give the value of:

   a the digit 6   b the digit 4.

3. Copy and complete these calculations.

   a 344.62 - 13.4 =   b 3400 - 257.66 =
   c 405.06 + 17.6 - 245.085 =

4. Two numbers have a difference of 387. One of the numbers is 75, what is the other number?

5. Copy and complete:

   a 3.85 × 6 =   b 16.47 × 7 =
   c 66.16 ÷ 8 =   d 0.007461 ÷ 3 =

6. a Find the sum of these numbers.
        5.72   12.08   16.65
   b Give the answer to 1dp.

7. Copy and complete:

   a 1.575 × 100 =   b 0.00675 × 10000 =
   c 124.55 ÷ 1000 =   d 1.05 ÷ 100 =

8. Picnic cups are 46p each.
   Calculate the cost of 125 cups.

9. A pack of six batteries costs £5.22
   Find the cost of one of these batteries.

10. Copy and complete:

    a 12 - 17 =   b 9 - ■ = 14

11. Find:
    a $3/5$ of 35 cards   b $5/8$ of 96 cans.

12. Which of these are **not** equivalent to $3/4$?

    $30/50$, $15/20$, $40/60$, $24/32$

13. Convert each to decimal and a percentage.

    a $14/100$ b $9/100$ c $3/4$

14. Which is larger: $3/4$ or $5/8$? Explain.

HOMEWORK R4

1. For each sequence, give the next three terms.

   a 1, 4, 7, 10, ...   b 3, 6, 9, 12, ...
   c 3, 7, 11, 15, ...   d $1/3$, $1/9$, $1/27$, ...

2. a What is the 21st square number?
   b Is 525 a square number?
      Explain how you decided.

3. Is 55 a triangle number?
   Explain how you decided.

4. The rule for the next term in a sequence is:

   subtract 5

   The sequence starts: 12, 7, 2, ...
   Copy and complete the sequence for the first six terms.

5. Write a rule for the sequence: ⁻11, ⁻7, ⁻3, ...

6. Give a rule for this number machine.

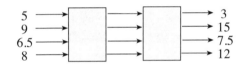

7. The cost C of a video tape is found by adding:
      the cost of the tape, t
      the cost of the box, b
      the cost of the packaging, p

   Write a formula that begins: C = ...

8. A group of n people play the lottery and share any prize w equally. Each player gets £p.

   Calculate the value of p when:
      $n = 8$, and $w = £6.8$ million.

9. With the formula $k = (a - b + c) \times 3$, find the value of k when $a = 5.8$, $b = 6.5$, and $c = 12.4$

10. A formula for the perimeter, P, of a rectangle of length a and width b is: $P = 2 \times (a + b)$.

    a Show how the formula is used to calculate the perimeter of a rectangle of length 13.8 cm and width 0.6 cm.
    b Write and use a formula for the area, A.

HOMEWORK R5

1. Collect like terms in each of these expressions.

   a $w + w + 3w - 4w$ **b** $18k - 11k$
   c $a + 3b + 5a$ **d** $9k + 3n - k$
   e $8n + 4 - n - 3$ **f** $5b - 4a + 3 + 9a$

2. Rewrite these, showing the hidden terms.

   a $7w + 4a - \blacksquare - \blacksquare = 4w + 3a$
   b $\blacksquare + \blacksquare - \blacksquare + 3k - h = 4h + 4k - n$
   c $3y - \blacksquare - \blacksquare - g + 8 = 2y - 5g + 8$
   d $\blacksquare + 4 + 6h - p - \blacksquare - \blacksquare = 5h + 4p - 2$

3. If $p = 5$, $k = 2$, and $g = 7$, give the value of:

   a $9k$ **b** $13g - 5$ **c** $8p - 5g$
   d $p + k - g$ **e** $9k - p - g$
   f $1.5p - 4k + 0.5g$ **g** $25 - 3p - 4.5k + g$

4. Give the value of each of these when:

   $w = 3$, $y = 4$, and $t = 2.5$

   a wy **b** wt **c** yt **d** wyt
   e $2t + 3wy$ **f** $5y - wy + 1$
   g $wt - y + 2ty$ **h** $25t - 2wy - ty$

5. Give the value of each of these when:

   $p = 4$, $r = 5$, and $u = 3$

   a p^2 **b** $u^2 - 4$ **c** r^2
   d $8r - p^2$ **e** $\frac{1}{2}u^2$ **f** p^3
   g $pr - ru$ **h** $2ru - u^2$ **i** $0.5pr$

HOMEWORK R6

1. Solve these equations.

   a $9y = 108$ **b** $6k = 54$
   c $\frac{1}{4}w = 16$ **d** $0.5p = 3.5$

2. Solve these equations.

   a $y + 3 = 24$ **b** $k - 8 = 24$
   c $4.8 + v = 14$ **d** $w - 650 = 500000$

3. Solve these equations.

   a $4y + 3 = 19$ **b** $55 + 3t = 121$
   c $8n - 15 = 17$ **d** $2.5k - 3 = 7$
   e $14y - 8 = 132$ **f** $7 + 1.5d = 19$

4. For each of these puzzles, write an equation and solve it to find the start number.

   a Start with a number, double it, then subtract 8.
   The answer is 2.
   b Start with a number, divide it by seven, then add 9.
   The answer is 15.
   c Start with a number, multiply by three, then add 4.
   The answer is 13.

5. Solve the equation $9w - 4 = 41$ by trial and improvement. Show all your working.
   You could use a table

6. What is the inverse of each of these?

   a subtract 17 **b** divide by 4

7. Draw the inverse of this number machine.

8. Draw a number machine to show how you can solve this puzzle.

   Start with a number, divide by 8, then subtract 5. The answer is 2.5
   What is the start number?

HOMEWORK R7

1. A shape has four sides of equal length. Its opposite sides are parallel.
   Name two shapes it could be.

2. This paving is made from two sizes of square paving slab.

   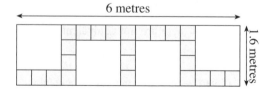

   Calculate the dimensions of each size of slab.

3 What is the order of rotational symmetry of this shape?

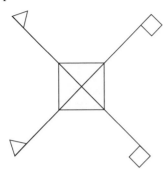

4 Calculate the sizes of angles *a* to *d*.

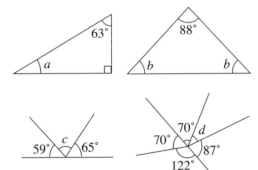

5 Construct a triangle with sides of 6.4 cm, 7.5 cm and 10.2 cm.

6 Which of these sets of dimensions can **not** be the lengths of the sides of a triangle?

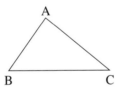

   a AB = 6 cm, BC = 4 cm, AC = 3 cm
   b AB = 8 cm, BC = 4 cm, AC = 3 cm
   c AB = 5 cm, BC = 11 cm, AC = 6 cm
   d AB = 4 cm, BC = 4 cm, AC = 7.5 cm

7 A rectangular garden is 17.2 metres long, and has an area of 216.72 square metres.

   a How wide is the garden?
   b Calculate its perimeter.

8 How long is it, in hours and minutes, between 10:35 am and 2:25 pm?

Homework R8

1 List the co-ordinates of points A to G.

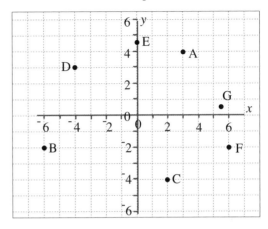

2 Copy this shape and draw in all its lines of symmetry.

3 a Measure angle *a* to the nearest degree.

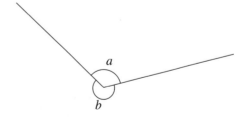

   b Calculate the size of angle *b*.

4 Draw accurately and label an angle of 167°.

5 A 50p piece has a thickness of about 3.2 mm. Give this thickness in centimetres.

6 Give each ratio in its lowest terms:

  a 12 : 56   b 15 : 135   c 420 : 35

7 Aisha, Jade and Mary share £672 in the ratio
      3 : 4 : 5
   How much does person receive?

8 A fruit drink is made from, orange, lemon, lime, and passion fruit juices.
   To make 250 litres of the fruit drink they use:
   90 l of orange, 25 l of lemon, 55 l of lime, and 80 l of passion fruit juice.

  a How much of each type of juice is needed to make 15550 litres of fruit drink?
  In making a different amount of the fruit drink 885 l of lemon juice was used.

  b How much of each other juice was used?

9 Calculate the area of this triangle.

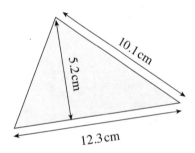

10 A trench, 40 cm deep, is dug in the ground for the foundations of a wall.

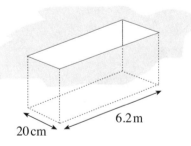

Calculate the surface area of all five inside faces of the trench.
Give your answer in m².

HOMEWORK R9

1 Name the solid that is made from this net.

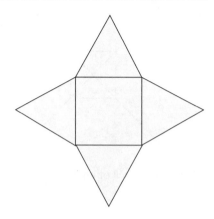

2 Draw the net of a box which measures 3 cm by 4 cm by 5 cm.

3 The fuel consumption of a new car is given as 47 miles per gallon.
   Use   1 gallon = 4.536 litres   to convert the fuel consumption to miles per litre.

4 What reading is shown on this scale?

5 a Calculate the area of this car park.

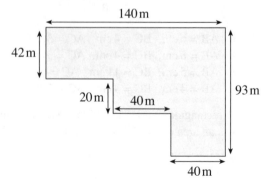

  b A chain is to be placed around the perimeter of the car park.
     What length of chain is needed?

6 Calculate angles *a* and *b* in this triangle.

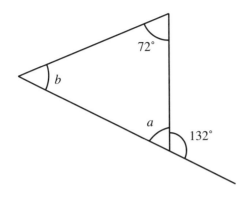

7 Convert 4.01 metres to:

  a centimetres   **b** millimetres.

8 a Construct a triangle with sides of 7.2 cm, 6.5 cm and 6.5 cm.

  b What name do we give this type of triangle?

9 How many lines of symmetry has:

  a a square?   **b** a rhombus?

10 Draw a shape with an order of rotational symmetry of 4.

HOMEWORK R10

1 Sarah made a list of the birds she saw in the garden.

Bird Survey

House Sparrow   Starling   Song Thrush
Starling   Starling   Chaffinch   Starling
Starling   House Sparrow   Starling
Blackbird   Robin   House Sparrow   Robin
Starling   Chaffinch   House Sparrow
House Sparrow   Song Thrush   Blackbird
Chaffinch   Song Thrush   House Sparrow
Black bird   House Sparrow   Blackbird

  a Make a frequency table to show this data.
  b How many birds did Sarah see altogether?
  c How many blackbirds did she see?

2 a Draw a bar-line graph to show Sarah's data.
  b Which bird, or birds, is the mode?

3

Breeds of Finch		
Name	Number of eggs	Incubation (days)
Bullfinch	4 - 5	12 - 14
Chaffinch	4 - 5	11 - 13
Greenfinch	4 - 6	13 - 14
Goldfinch	5 - 6	12 - 13
Hawfinch	4 - 6	9.5

  a How many eggs does the chaffinch lay?
  b For how many days does the bullfinch incubate its eggs?
  c If you found a finch's nest, what do you think would be the most likely number of eggs in it?
  d On average, which finch do you think incubates its eggs for longest? Explain.

4 Paul looks for finch nests in the hedgerows around a local farm.

Finch Egg Survey - Hall Farm
Number of eggs in each nest

6 5 5 4 4 5 4
4 4 5 6 6 5
4 5 5 6 5 6 4

  a How many nests did Paul find?
  b List the data in order.
  c Find the median number of eggs in a nest.
  d How many eggs did Paul find altogether?
  e Calculate the mean number of eggs.

5 Paul does a survey at another farm.

Finch Egg Survey - Oak Farm
Number of eggs in each nest

4 5 6 5 6 6
5 4 6 5 6 6
6 5 4 5

  a How many eggs did Paul find altogether?
  b Calculate the mean number of eggs.

6 Use your answers to questions **4** and **5** to compare the finch nests on the two farms.

7 Paul draws a bar chart to show the number of eggs found in the nests at the two farms.

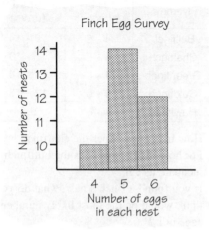

Finch Egg Survey

a How many nests contained 6 eggs?
b Ruth looks at Paul's chart and says that three times as many nests contained 6 eggs as 4 eggs.
Why do you think Ruth said that?
c Draw a better chart to show this data.

HOMEWORK R11

1 *Rushmoor Rockets* basketball team have an important play-off game.
Jordan and Neal are competing for a place in the team.

Jordan Byrd
Points scored in each game

| 15 | 17 | 7 | 23 | 22 |
| 6 | 18 | 24 | 29 | 15 |

Neal O'Leary
Points scored in each game

| 15 | 19 | 10 | 14 | 24 | 14 |
| 13 | 38 | 27 | 17 | 18 | |

a Calculate the range of the number of points scored by Jordan, and by Neal.
b For each player, calculate the mean number of points scored per game.
c Find the median number of points for each player.

2 Why is the median a better average to use to compare these scores than the mean?

3 a Use the values for the median and the range from question **1** to compare the two players.
b Which player would you pick for the team? Explain how you decided.

4 These are the points scored by the *Rushmoor Rockets* in their games in the 1997 season.

Points scored by Rushmoor Rockets

81	94	88	70	66	87	79
98	104	83	99	76	106	80
96	86	78	100	86	97	104
88	101	67	91	83	106	71

a Copy and complete the tally chart below to show this data.

Rushmoor Rockets

Points	Tally	Total
60 - 69		
70 - 79		
80 - 89		
90 - 99		
100 - 109		
	Grand Total	

b How many games did *Rushmoor Rockets* play in the 1997 season?
c Which was the modal group of points?
d Draw a bar chart to show this data.

5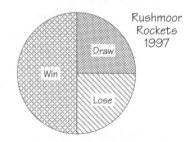

Rushmoor Rockets 1997

a How many games did *Rushmoor Rockets* win in the 1997 season?
b How many games did they lose?

6 In the 1996 season, the *Rushmoor Rockets* played 32 games.

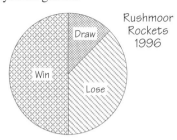

a How many games did *Rushmoor Rockets* win in the 1996 season?

b How many games do you think they drew?

HOMEWORK R12

1 *Cinders Athletics Club* has 6 junior members: Aisha, Beth, Colin, Daley, Eve and Frank.
Of these athletes, Colin (C) is:
  3rd fastest at 400 metres,
  2nd fastest at 1500 metres.

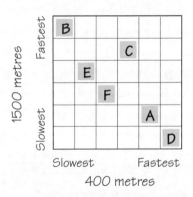

a Copy and complete this sentence:
  Aisha (A) is ___ fastest at 400 metres,
        and ___ fastest at 1500 metres.

b Who is faster at 400 m, Eve or Frank?

c Who is slower at 1500 m, Colin or Eve?

d Describe the link that the diagram shows between the athletes' speeds in the 400 m and their speeds in the 1500 m.

e Which athlete does this link not apply to quite as well as the others?

2   0%   50%   100%

a Copy this scale.

b Estimate the chance that each of the following things will happen and show them on your scale.

  A You will live to be 100

  B You will remember your dream when you wake up tomorrow

  C It will be sunny tomorrow

3 The weather forecaster estimates there is a 25% chance of rain tomorrow.
What is the forecaster's estimate of the chance of it **not** raining tomorrow?

4 Dina flips a coin three times and gets a head followed by two tails.
If she flips the coin once more, what is the probability she will get a head?

5 A game uses a special roller dice. The numbers on the dice are:

  2   3   5   7   11   13

Give the probability of scoring:

a 7   **b** more than 10
c 3 or more   **d** an odd number
e an even number   **f** a prime number.

6 Peta holds a raffle in aid of Comic Relief. The details of the raffle are:

  Number of prizes donated   10
  Number of tickets sold   50
  No ticket can win more than 1 prize

John buys one ticket.

a What is the probability he will win a prize?

b What is the probability John will win the first prize?

c If John does not win first or second prize, what is the probability he will win the third prize?

HOMEWORK R13

1. List the first five multiples of 12.

2. A set of three prime numbers has a sum of 26.

   a Find three sets of 3 primes with this sum.
   b For each set find its product.
   c Which set has the largest range?

3. Two consecutive numbers have a product of 756. Find the sum of the two numbers.

4. A soccer pitch is 90.1 metres long and a squash court is 9.75 metres long. Without using a calculator, find the difference between these lengths.

5. Without using a calculator, work out the value of 0.0564×10000.

6. 40% of the 1250 people in a survey did not own a bike.

   a What percentage owned a bike?
   b How many did not own a bike?

7. Collect like terms in this expression.

   $3a + 6 - b + 5 + 3b - 2a - 8b + c - 12$

8. If $p = 4$, $q = ^-16$, $r = 12$ and $s = 24$, give the value of:

   a $2s - 3q$ b $pr - s$
   c $100 - pq$ d $\tfrac{1}{2}r^2 - s$

9. Solve the equation: $\tfrac{1}{2}p - 18 = 7$

10. Copy and complete this number machine to solve the equation: $7d - 3 = 81$.

    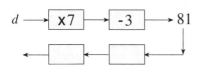

11. A straight line passes through the points $(4, ^-3)$ and $(2, ^-3)$.
    Give the co-ordinates of the point where the line crosses the y-axis.

12. Without using a calculator find $\sqrt{15}$.
    Give your answer to 3dp.

13. a Construct a triangle with sides of 3.9 cm, 5.2 cm and 6.5 cm.
    b What name do we give this type of triangle?

14. A cuboid has a surface area of 288 cm². Its length is three times its width and is also twice its height. Use trial and improvement to find its height, length and width.

HOMEWORK R14

1. Copy and complete each of these.

   a $^-3 + 7 =$ b $5 + ^-7 =$
   c $^-6 - 4 =$ d $^-2 + ^-4 =$
   e $^-5 - ^-2 =$ f $^-8 - ^-10 =$

2. Anton buys seven films and has one set of prints developed at £4.59
   The total comes to £28.74
   Calculate the cost of one film.

3. Use the formula $s = (p - 2q) \times 5.2$ to calculate the value of s when:

   a $p = 12$ and $q = 4$ b $p = 9.4$ and $q = 2.3$

4. If $p = 12$ and $f = 5$, copy and complete each of these.

   a $fp - \blacksquare = 45$ b $f(p + f) + \blacksquare = 93$
   c $p(f + \blacksquare) = 132$ d $f^2 + p^2 - \blacksquare = 122$

5. a A shape has four sides.
      Only one pair of opposite sides is parallel.
      What name do we give the shape?
   b How many sides has a heptagon?

6. The digits 3, 4, 5, 6, 8 and 9 can be put, one in each box, to make this sum correct.

   Show how the digits can be placed.

7. a Calculate the area of this parallelogram.

   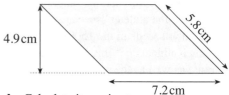

   b Calculate its perimeter.

8 A cuboid has two faces with an area of 20 cm², two faces with an area of 28 cm², and two faces with an area of 35 cm².

  a Find the dimensions of the cuboid.
  b Sketch the cuboid showing its dimensions.

9 How long is it between each of these times?

  a 12:45 and 16:22
  b 10:55 am and 3:12 pm
  c 9:26 pm and 1:55 am
  d 23:16 and 00:56

10 For this set of numbers, calculate:

  12, 16, 21, 18, 4, 3, 4, 17, 146, 22

  a the mean   **b** the mode
  c the median **d** the range

HOMEWORK R15

1 This pie chart shows the sales of items of clothing in a shop one Saturday.

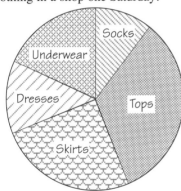

Altogether, 640 items were sold on that day.
  a Roughly how many skirts were sold?
  b 85 of one item were sold.
       Which item was it?
  c What fraction of the items sold were tops?

2 I think of a number, multiply it by 3 then add 4.6 and the answer is 16.

  Explain how you find:
  a the number I first thought of
  b the answer when the start number is 8.5
  c the answer when the start number is 0.018

3 What decimal is $7/100$ larger than 3.267?

4 In a police survey of 240 bikes:
  $3/5$ were owned by people under 20
  $5/8$ were bought within the last two years
  $1/3$ had dangerously-worn tyres
  160 had faulty brakes.

  a How many bikes had been bought within the last two years?
  b What fraction of the bikes had faulty brakes?
  c How many more bikes had faulty brakes than dangerously-worn tyres?
  d What fraction of the bikes in the survey were owned by people aged 20 or older?

5 For each sequence, give the next three terms.

  a 7, 11, 15, 19, …
  b 128, 64, 32, 16, …
  c 0.2, 0.4, 0.6, 0.8, …
  d 128, 112, 96, 80, …

6 What reading is shown on this scale?

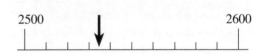

7 Calculate the area of this shape.

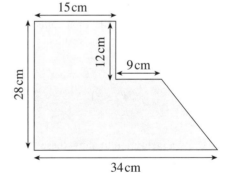

8 Square tiles of side 45 mm are used to tile part of a wall. The tiles must cover a section that is 29.75 cm wide and 2.7 metres long.

What is the smallest number of tiles that can be used to cover the section?

HOMEWORK R16

1 How many lines of symmetry has each of these shapes?

   a a regular hexagon   **b** a rhombus
   c a kite   **d** a scalene triangle
   e an isosceles triangle   **f** a regular pentagon

2 For this set of numbers, calculate:

   134, 1247, 32, 6, 92, 21, 134, 32

   a the mean   **b** the median
   c the mode   **d** the range

3 Without using a calculator, work out the value of each of these.

   a 4.532×100 **b** 2.6×100000
   c 0.00416×10000 **d** 123.74×1000
   e $45.7 \div 100$ **f** $1.0046 \div 10000$
   g 14.23×400000 **h** $0.64 \div 2000$

4 Solve these equations.

   a $7g + 9 = 65$ **b** $4a - 56 = 72$
   c $3b - 45 = 111$ **d** $67 + 8h = 119$
   e $3f - 5 = 34$ **f** $5k - 7 = 134$

5 **a** Construct a triangle with sides of 10 cm, 15.5 cm and 11 cm.
   b Measure the interior angles, and give the size of each angle to the nearest degree.

6 Jessica asks 20 pupils what coins they have on them. These are the results.

   Coin Survey - 20 pupils

1p	2p	5p	10p	20p	50p	£1
16	14	18	19	25	15	17

Draw a pictogram to show these results, using this key.

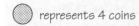 represents 4 coins

7 A cuboid measures 3 cm by 4.5 cm by 6 cm.

   a Draw a net of this cuboid.
   b Calculate the total area of the net.

HOMEWORK R17

1 When you roll a normal dice, what is the probability of scoring:

   a less than 5?   **b** a factor of 10?
   c a multiple of 3?   **d** a prime number?

2 I think of a number, multiply by 3 then take 5. The answer is 46. Find the start number.

3 For this puzzle, write an equation and then solve it to find the starting number.

> You have a number, you double it, then subtract six. The answer is 35.

4 Copy each of these and, where necessary, put in brackets to make the answer correct.

   a $70 \div 7 - 2 = 14$ **b** $70 \div 7 - 2 = 8$
   c $2 + 5 \times 3 = 17$ **d** $2 + 5 \times 3 = 21$
   e $4 \times 8 + 6 \div 2 = 28$ **f** $4 \times 8 + 6 \div 2 = 35$
   g $4 \times 8 + 6 \div 2 = 19$ **h** $24 \div 6 - 2 \times 2 = 0$

5 In this diagram, lines AB and CD are parallel.

Calculate the sizes of the labelled angles.
Do not measure the angles

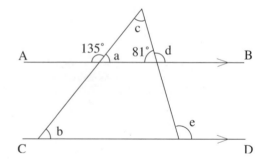

6 Coach A leaves London at 9:42 am and reaches Newcastle at 3:02 pm.
Coach B leaves London at 11:13 am and takes $5\tfrac{1}{4}$ hours to reach Newcastle.

   a Write the times for coach A in 24-hour time.
   b How long after coach A leaves does coach B leave?
   c Which coach takes the shorter time, and how much quicker is it?